A Description Of The King's Royal Palace And Gardens At Loo: Together With A Short Account Of Holland

Walter Harris

In the interest of creating a more extensive selection of rare historical book reprints, we have chosen to reproduce this title even though it may possibly have occasional imperfections such as missing and blurred pages, missing text, poor pictures, markings, dark backgrounds and other reproduction issues beyond our control. Because this work is culturally important, we have made it available as a part of our commitment to protecting, preserving and promoting the world's literature. Thank you for your understanding.

A DESCRIPTION OF The KING's Royal Palace AND Gardens at *LOO*.

TOGETHER

With a Short Account of *HOLLAND*.

In which

There are some Observations relating to their DISEASES.

By *WALTER HARRIS*, M. D. Physician in Ordinary to His MAJESTY, and Fellow of the College of Physicians.

LONDON:
Printed by *K. Roberts*, and Sold by *T. Nutt*, near Stationers Hall. MDCXCIX.

THE PREFACE.

THIS *Description of the King's Palace*, and *Gardens* at *Loo*, was most of it written at the Command of our late most *Incomparable Queen, of ever Glorious Memory*, who was not displeased with the Sight of it; and who, tho' she Honoured this *Royal Fabrick* with the laying its *first Stone*, yet could never have the Pleasure of seeing it Perfected: The *Wise* and *Good Queen's* Presence being, during the War, most Necessary within the Kingdom, whilst His *Majesty* exposed His *Royal Person* in the Field, for the Preservation of us all, and for the Benefit of Mankind; and did so eminently signalize himself Abroad, that all the *Martial Virtues* which are reported in History to have belong'd unto any the most Renowned of the *Roman* or *Grecian Heroes*, have been evidently conspicuous, and United together in His *Majesty*.

Since this *Description* was first written, it has been Corrected and Enlarged, by the frequent Opportunities I have had, of walking over the Gardens, in the five Years time that I had the Honour to wait upon His *Majesty* Abroad. And the Reading it must give some Diversion to the Curious, as the Writing it was pleasing to me. Also *Persons of Quality*, and *Great Fortunes*, may here find many things to *Admire*, and also to *Imitate*, if they please, when they are taking their Summer Diversions at their Country Seats.

As for what I add, in the *Account of Holland*, I shall only tell you, I considered that a *Description* cannot possibly represent things with that Pleasure and Advantage, as they are Seen upon the Place; and I thought a few *Common Observations* I made in *Holland*, and which I have recollected upon the *Printing* this *Description*, would not be unacceptable to some *Persons*, for *Variety sake*; tho' I have been guilty of many *Omissions*, rather than I would be tedious, by *Consulting Authors*, or reciting any of their *Observations*, who have taken Pains upon this Subject, and been more large and accurate in their Performances.

A TABLE of the CHAPTERS.

THE *Introduction.*

CHAP. I. *Of the Situation of the* Palace *and* Gardens. *Of the* Court *before the* Palace. *A short view of the* Palace *it self; and a summary Account of all the* Gardens *in General.*

CHAP. II. *A Description of the* Great Garden, *next behind the* Palace; *and first of that part of it, call'd the* Lower-Garden.

CHAP. III. *Of the second part of the* Great Garden, *call'd the* Upper Garden: *Together with the Middle Walk, and* Canals, *which do divide this* Garden *into the* Two Parts.

CHAP. IV. *Of the* King's Garden, *and, Westward of it, a* Labyrinth, *or* Wilderness.

CHAP. V. *Of the* Queen's Garden, *and another* Wilderness, *beyond it Eastward.*

CHAP. VI. *Of the* Voliere, *or* Fowl-Garden.

CHAP. VII. *Of the* Park, *and its* Fountains, Canal, Cascade, &c. *Of the* Viver, *that supplies the* Fountains, Cascades, *and* Canals, *with Water. Also a Description of* six other Vivers, *or* Fishponds.

A Short Account of HOLLAND.

The CONTENTS.

THat the Gardens at Loo were finished during the War; when the French King put a stop to all Publick Works. *The occasion of this Account. Of the Courage of the* Low-Country Men. *A preference of the* English *to all others in that respect. Their preference in former times. In* Turenne's *time. At the Siege of* Namur. *Of how great Consideration the Goodness of a* General *is to an* Army. *A remarkable Instance of it in the Revolution that happened in* 1672. *Of the Unanimity of the* Dutch. *Their great Deference to His Majesty's Wisdom. Of the Province of* Holland *more particularly. The* Low-Countries *why so called. Of the* Canals *in* Holland. *Their Water not offensive. No Variety of Objects to be seen in the Country. A recommendation of the Country about* Dort. *Of the* Dutch Brabant. *Of a Noble Seat near* Zutphen. *Of* Zealand. *The good Effects that* Travelling *abroad has, or ought to have. How a Traveller ought to Demean himself in* Holland. *Of their* Taxes. *Of their* Justice. *Their* Musick-Houses *at* Amsterdam. *Of their* Food, Beer, *and* Wines. *Of their* Diseases. *And particularly their* Fevers *and* Agues. *Of their* Phlebotomy. *Why the* Dutch *have so few* Coughs, *and we so many. Of their* Provision *for the* Poor. *Of their* Charity *in* Churches. *Their* Apparel. *In what respect the* Dutch *do deserve great Consideration from us. A remarkable Observation of the Emperor* Charles *the Fifth, against* Bigotry. *A strict* Alliance, *and good Understanding between* England *and* Holland, *never more necessary than at present.*

A

A

Description of His MAJESTY's Palace and Gardens at *LOO*.

Together, with

Some Account of the People and Country.

The INTRODUCTION.

NOTHING does give Posterity so Noble an Idea of former Times, as the *Magnificence* of their *Buildings*. The Remains we still have of the *Roman* Greatness in their Publick Structures are enough to merit our highest admiration. The Ruins of their *Amphitheatres* as they are now to be seen, their immense *Obelisks*, their prodigious *Aquæducts*, their splendid *Palaces* and *Temples*, their subterranean *Catacombs*, and even their *Via Appia*, and *Flaminea*, or their *Causeways* that were made near Two thousand Years ago, when *Rome* was a *Republick*, with a Stone so hard, and so firmly laid, as still to remain entire a good way in many Places, are all Objects so conspicuous, and so durable in their kinds, that some of them are like to continue to the end of the World everlasting Monuments of the just Veneration due to Ancient Times, of their admirable Skill, if not Perfection in *Architecture*; and in a word, as undoubted Testimonies of the *Splendour* and *Magnificence* of the *Greatest People* that ever were recorded in *History*.

What can give us such a representation of the Pomp and Grandeur of the *Kings* of *Ægypt*, as the Wonderful *Pyramids* there to be seen, and the illustrious Ruins of *Grand Cairo* and *Alexandria*!

Our *English* indeed have bestowed their Munificence chiefly in lasting Monuments of their Piety, in erecting abundance of the Noblest *Cathedrals* that can anywhere be seen. And *England* may deservedly glory not only in the stately *Cathedrals* she has built at home, as well as in her

Palaces,

Palaces, Universities, and other Publick and Private Buildings, but hath left in *France* the lasting Evidences of her *Magnificence,* by erecting those stately *Nostredames* at *Paris,* at *Amiens,* at *Rouen,* &c. at a time when great part of *France* was under the *English Dominion,* and when the rest of it did as much dread the *English Power* and *Courage,* as themselves have of late Years been a Terror to all their Neighbours. Nay, at this present time, by the *Publick Authority* (to our Honour and Renown be it spoken) there is now erecting, and almost finished, in her *Metropolis,* one of the most spacious and *Magnificent Cathedrals* that ever yet was built in the World; and the which, in the judgment of Travellers, is like to emulate in its Structure, even *Saint Peter's* at *Rome,* and *Sancta Sophia* at *Constantinople.*

His *Majesty* is possessed of many Noble and Stately *Palaces* both at Home and Abroad. *Kensington* and *Hampton-Court* are too well known to be more than mentioned. His *Castle of Windsor* may dispute for Excellency in many respects with most of the *Royal Palaces* in *Europe.* And at *Winchester* there is another of His *Majesty's Palaces,* in a most admirable Situation for *Health* as well as *Pleasure,* that wants but little of being finished. I cannot but wish this last were nearer to *London,* or were thereby better situated for His *Majesty's* Convenience. For I have sensibly experienced the benefit of that Healthful Situation, having had the Happiness to be Educated in the *College* at *Winchester;* where in Seven Years time I never knew one of the Seventy Children of that College to die, altho' it be seated in the lowest, and consequently the most unhealthy part of that City. And others have assured me, that in Fifty Years past, there have not died above four or five of that Excellent Seminary of Learning, and most of those too by Violent Accidents, not by Epidemical Diseases. The which is a Consideration worthy of the thoughts of such Parents, who would do their utmost to preserve their Posterity, and are desirous to breed their Children in the *best School* in *England.*

In the *Low Countries,* in *Brabant,* and elsewhere, His *Majesty's* Ancient Hereditary Palaces are dispersed in great number. The *Royal Palace* and *Gardens* at *Loo* are the Subject of the ensuing Discourse. I will only mention *Dieren,* an Ancient Seat of the most *Illustrious House* of *Nassaw,* five Leagues from *Loo*; *Honslaer-Dike,* two Leagues from the *Hague*; *Soestdike,* not far from *Utrecht,* the Castle of *Breda,* made much more Illustrious of late by his *Majesty*; *Ryswick* the auspicious Place of Treaty of Peace, and now rendred everlastingly famous by the Conclusion of a *Peace* so Happy and so Honourable to the greatest part of *Europe.* All which *Palaces* (except the last, where the King has never resided, it being so near the *Hague*) do remain nobly furnished for His *Majesty's* Reception, and have *Gardens* belonging to them that might merit a distinct Description.

For *Buildings* of themselves, howsoever Noble and Great, do appear very deficient without the Ornament and Conveniencies of a *Garden.* *Italy,* the *Garden* of the *World,* and the great Repository of Rarities

and

and Antiquities, does now as much glory and pride her self in the Pomp, and Ornaments, and Conveniencies belonging to her *Gardens*, as in any of her so much celebrated Curiosities. It is certainly one of the most innocent and sweetest Diversions that can be desired; it gives easie opportunities for Retirement and Contemplation, and conduces to the obtaining a chearful Tranquillity of Mind, and to the preservation of a healthful Temper of Body. It is a delight and satisfaction to which some of the *Greatest Princes* and *Noblemen* in all Ages have had recourse, after they had been satiated and cloy'd with the Pleasures and Vanities of the World, or had been tired with the Crosses and Disappointments, the Vexations and Troubles, which do necessarily attend all Conditions of Life. And if there be any tolerable share of *Happiness* and *Content* to be any where enjoyed by an Innocent Man, out of the hurry and noise of the World, a compleat and spacious *Garden*, furnished with variety of *Walks* and *Groves*, and adorned with *Fountains, Cascades, Grottoes*, &c. must do very much towards the obtaining even a *Paradise* upon Earth.

The Gardens of *Loo* are become so famous and remarkable to all the *Provinces* near them, that Curious Persons from divers Parts of *Germany*, as well as out of all the *United Provinces*, do frequently resort thither to satisfie their Curiosity. I will not here enlarge in their praise and admiration, but leave it to the Reader to make a true judgment of them from the *Description* it self, which is at least natural and plain, and as perspicuous as the nature of such *Descriptions* (sometimes necessarily intricate through the great variety of matter) will admit, tho' indeed very destitute of the Ornaments and Flourishes that are usually made in the describing Great Things, to make them appear *Greater* than they really are.

CHAP. I.

Of the Situation of the Palace *and* Gardens; *of the* Court *before the* Palace; *a short view of the* Palace *it self; and a summary Account of all the* Gardens *in general.*

HIS *Majesty's Palace* and *Gardens* at *Loo*, are situated on the East-side of a large Sandy *Heath*, or in the *Veluwe*, a considerable part of the Province of *Gelderland*, one of the *Seven United Provinces*. The *Heath* is extended Southward unto the *Rhine*, and Northward unto the *Zuyder*, or *South Sea*; Westward it runs almost to *Amersfort*, or within less than two Leagues of it; and Eastward it is extended to the *Issel*, a considerable River that divides *Overyssell* from the *Veluwe*. *Loo* is three Leagues from *Deventer*, five from *Harderwick* on the South-Sea, five from *Dieren*; another of His *Majesty's Palaces*, six from *Arnheim*, and twelve Leagues or Hours from *Utrecht*. It is an excellent Country for *Hunting*, and abounds with *Staggs*, some *Roe-bucks*, the Wild *Boar, Foxes, Hares,*

Hares, and some *Wolfs*. It is no less excellent for *Fowling*, and has good store of *Woodcocks, Partridges, Pheasants*, &c. In a Wood near *Loo*, there is a *Herniary* for Hawking, and within a League of it North-east, His *Majesty* has of late caused to be made an Excellent *Decoy*, which supplies his Family with good store of *Ducks* and *Teale*. And in the *Heath* beyond the *Gardens*, there are six *Vivers*, or large *Fish-ponds*, somewhat after the model or resemblance of those in *Hide-Park*, the one communicating with the other. You will find them described at the end of this Treatise, in the Seventh Chapter.

The *New Palace*, lately built by His *Majesty*, is near unto the *Old Hoof*, or *Old Court*, which is a *Castle* surrounded with a broad Moat, and purchased about 12 or 14 Years ago from the *Seigneur de Laeckhuysen*, a Gentleman of this Country. They are separated from one another only by some of the *Gardens*, which lie on the West-side of the *New Palace*. The *Gardens* are most Sumptuous and Magnificent, adorned with great variety of most Noble *Fountains, Cascades, Parterres, Gravel Walks*, and *Green Walks, Groves, Statues, Urns, Paintings, Seats*, and pleasant Prospects into the Country.

Before the *Gate* that enters into the *Court* of the *Palace*, there is a broad Green *Walk* between a double row of Oaks, half a Mile long; and at the end of this Walk next to the *Heath*, there is a *Gate* of Iron Rails between double Stone *Pillars* of an *Ancient* Model, the *Pillars* being about a Yard distant from each other, and joined at the top by a *Crown Work* on each side, wherein is cut His *Majesty's Cypher*, and at the bottom by a Stone Ground-work, or *Supporters*. The *Columns* are of a good heighth. Before this Gate there are *three Walks* between *Trees* for a Mile, or more, farther into the *Heath*.

On the South-side of the *Palace*, we do enter through a large *Gate* of Iron Bars, painted Blue and Gilded, into a *Quadrangular Court*, of which the whole South-side hath Iron Rails alike Painted and Gilded. The Rails are placed on a low Brick Wall that is covered with Free-stone the whole length, five Inches above the Brick. Among these Iron Rails, which do rise above eight Foot higher than the Wall, these are at due distances 28 *Pilasters*, every one of them of *one entire Stone*. The East-side of the *Court* does contain Offices and Chambers for the *Officers* and Servants of His *Majesty's Houshold*.

On the West-side of the *Court* are the *King's Stables*, and in these are kept *Horses* for His *Majesty's own Riding*. And at the end of this *Stable*, adjoining to the Rails before-mentioned, there is another *double Stable* for His *Majesty's other Horses*, and for those of some of his Servants, extended Westward about 80 Paces on the Road that comes from *Utrecht*. At the other end of the Rails, or adjoining to the East-side of the *Court*, upon the Road, there is another Row of *Building*, in proportion to the *Stables*, containing a Guard-house, a large *Orangery*, or Green-house, the *King's Coach-houses*, &c.

In

[5]

In the middle of the *Court* there is a *Fountain*, whose Basin consists of a wrought blue Stone, and whose Stone-work is raised two Foot and a half high. In the middle of this *Fountain* there are four Marble *Dolphins*, out of whose Mouths do fall four Sheets of Water, to the East, West, North, and South. The *Dolphins* are placed upon a Marble Pedestal; their Tails are intertwisted, and turned upward in the middle of the Pedestal. But this *Fountain* has been ordered to be changed into a Noble *Cascade*, in an octangular Basin, seven yards Diameter. Next unto the Walk that encompasses this *Fountain*, there are in this *Court* four *Gazons*, or Green Plots, with Walks on every side paved with Brick.

On the North-side of the *Court* is the *King's Palace*, to which we ascend by nine broad Stone-steps. The *Palace* is built of Brick, and had the Honour to have the first Stone laid by the hands of the most *Incomparable* and *Best* of *Queens*, her late *Majesty* of ever Blessed Memory. From the *Front*, or *Body* of the *House*, each *Wing* does stretch out in two *Pavilions* towards the two sides of the *Court*, until the *Wings* and *Sides* do come to unite. Besides the *Gate* in the middle of the *Front*, there are two others in the two outmost *Pavilions*. Over the Gate of the Front, and the Garden-Gate, and over the two outmost *Pavilions*, there are *Frontispieces*, or *Relievos* on high, with Representations relating to *Hunting*. The *Pilasters* of all the Gates or Doors, the *Frize*, and the *Cornishes* of the Windows, do consist of Free-stone. The *Body* of the *Palace* is Leaded above, and adorned with Ballisters; and it has large Shash-Windows throughout. The *Hall* we do first enter into, is paved with very large Black and White Marble. The *Dining-Room* below is very remarkable throughout, and especially in its *Marble* and Military *Devices*, and glorious *Gilding*. The *Great-Room* above, that we do first enter into from the *Stair-case*, and in the middle of the Apartments, is not only adorned with large *Landskips*, as well as the *Stair-case*, but is very resplendent with its *Gilding* on every side, and throughout all the *Cieling*. The *Rooms* of State, and the *Bed-Chambers*, and other *Chambers*, are all provided and furnished after the Noblest manner, for the Entertainment and Reception of *Great Persons*. But the *Anti-chamber* to His *Majesty's Bed-chamber* has most excellent *Hangings*, representing the Functions or Duties of *Cavalry*, to wit, the *Incampment* of *Horse*, their *Foraging*, their making of *Fascines*, and the *Firing* it self of two Parties of *Horse* in an Engagement, most lively and naturally exprest, in four several Pieces. The *Chappel* is handsomely Wainscoted, and the whole so compleatly finished, that nothing can be said to be wanting, and no Cost spared in order to render the *House Magnificent*, as well as the *Gardens*.

When we have gone through the *Hall* of the *Palace*, and advanced between a very large *Stair-case* on either hand, we do come to the *Garden-Gate*, which is directly before the Entrance, and consists of Iron Bars curiously wrought and painted.

B But

But before I describe particularly any of the *Gardens*, it may not be amiss to take a short and general Prospect of them, as also to name some of the most remarkable *Fountains* and *Cascades* in them, that thereby the whole may in some of its Particulars be more distinctly comprehended.

On the North-side of the *Palace*, there is a large and most *Magnificent Garden*, the which is divided into two Parts, the *Lower-Garden*, and the *Upper*: The two Divisions being separated by *Canals*, by a low Wall, and a broad Cross-walk, in the which Cross-walk there are on each side a double row of tall Oaks; but in the middle of this Walk a considerable space is left open, without Trees, for the more convenient view of all the *Fountains*, the *Porticoes*, and the *Cascades*, that are beyond the said Walk, from the *Garden-Gate* of the *Palace*.

The first partition of this *Garden*, called the *Lower-Garden*, has a *Terras Walk* on three sides of it; and here we behold straight before us the *Fountain* of *Venus*, and beyond it another *Fountain* of a young *Hercules*. In the Cross-walk that goes between those two Fountains, there is on the right hand a Fountain of a *Celestial Globe*, and on the left such another *Terrestrial Globe*. And at the end of the same Walk on the right hand, upon the side of one Terras Walk, there is the *Cascade* of *Narcissus*, as also on the left, upon the side of the opposite Terras Walk, the *Cascade* of *Galatea*.

In the *Upper Garden* we behold a most Noble Fountain, with a Basin of a vast extent, and with 33 *Spouts*, that in the middle of all throwing up the Water 45 foot high.

A little beyond this, we see another Fountain, wherein the Water rises in the form of a *Peacock's Tail*, under which, as also beyond it, are divers *Cascades*. We do likewise here behold two large *Porticoes*, or semicircular *Cloisters*, with Rails over them, and supported on divers Pillars.

On the West-side of the *Palace* there is a *Garden* under His *Majesty's Apartments*, and called the *King's Garden*. This has a Noble *Fountain* in the middle of it, and adjoyning to it there is a large *Bowling-Green*.

Beyond this *Garden* Westward, there is another called the *Labyrinth* or *Wilderness*, some of whose Fountains may be seen, as also Statues in it, and Painting, from His *Majesty's Bed-Chamber*.

On the East-side of the *Palace* there is another *Garden*, under the Apartments appointed for the *Queen*, and called the *Queen's Garden*. This bears a just proportion with that of the *King's*, and hath such another noble *Fountain*. And adjoyning to this *Garden* Southwards, there are divers *Arbor* Walks, with five Fountains in the middle of Parterres.

Beyond the Wall of the *Queen's Garden*, Eastward, there is another handsom *Garden* for Retirement, or a *Labyrinth*, answering the other, with Fountains, Statues, Walks, &c.

From the Cross-Walk that divides the *Upper* from the *Lower Garden*, behind the *Palace*, we go through Gates into the *Voliere*, or *Fowl-Garden*, West from those others. And still farther Westward we enter into a large

extent

extent of Ground, called the *Park*, wherein are to be seen the *Long Canal* with *Spouts* the whole length of it, all rising in the form of an *Arch*. Beyond this, is the *Cypher Fountain* and *Cascade*, and beyond that the *Viver*, or large Quadrangular Pond, which contains the Water that supplies the *Jette's*, and *Cascades*. Within this *Park* is also the Fountain of *Faunus*, divers pleasant and long green Walks, Nurseries of young Trees, Groves, and Canals; and West of the *Viver* there is a fine *Grove* for Solitude or Retirement, and call'd the *Queen's Grove*. Of all which now more at large.

CHAP. II.

Containing the Description of the Great Garden, *next behind the* Palace; *and first of that part of it called the* Lower Garden.

SO soon as we have pass'd through the *Palace*, we do enter upon a very broad *Terras-walk*, extended on the right and left the whole breadth of this Garden, the which is continued forwards by a Brick-wall, and by other Terras-walks on the right and left sides of it. The first Terras walk is paved with Brick 14 yards forwards, between the Garden-Gate and the Stone-steps, by which we are to descend into the Garden. It is also paved with Brick 30 paces both to the right and left. From the said paving, this Terras-walk is continued to the Garden-Walls on each side, in a green and gravel Walk. The middle part of this Walk is Green about 15 foot, and on each side of the Green there is a Gravel-walk, each of them 10 foot broad.

At both ends of this first Terras-walk we do ascend by seven Steps unto the side Terras-walks, which are raised higher than the former, for the better placing of those Noble Stone-Fabricks that compose the *Cascades* of *Narcissus* and *Galatea*. These Terras-walks do, like the former, consist of a Green-walk in the middle, and a Gravel-walk on each side of the Green. In the middle of these side Terras-walks, behind the *Cascades*, there are *Seats* next to the Walls, and painted Green.

From the first Terras-walk, near the *Garden-Gate* of the *Palace*, there is a very large descent into the *Garden*, first by three Semicircular Stone-steps, and after a little space by 15 Steps more, all of a very large Circumference, the lowermost of those 15 Steps being 28 *yards* round.

On the right side of the foresaid Steps, upon the Terras-walk, there is a large *Stone-Statue*, with a *Hart* behind it, and on the left such another great *Statue*, both lying or leaning on a distinct *Basis*, and both holding under one Arm a Stone-Vessel. These *Two Statues* are intended to represent two great *Rivers*, the *Rhine* and the *Yssel*, between the which Rivers, the *Veluwe*, and *Loo* are situate. Out of those Stone-Vessels there runs Water, which makes an *unexpected Cascade* on both sides of the *Steps* adjoyning to the Wall. These *Cascades* are made from the said Stone-Vessels, on each side, into seven double Basins, one below another,

ther, besides an eighth large single Basin, which receives the Water of all the rest, at the bottom of the Steps. All these Basins are of a blue Stone. The one half of these double Basins is raised two or three Inches, in order to retain the Water, and the other half is equally sunk or made lower, that the Sheet of Water may fall from the upper into the lower Basins.

From all the three Terras-Walks, there is a Green Slope, reaching from those Walks above unto a low Brick-Wall below, that is only two Foot high; at the four corners of these Slopes, in this Garden, there are broad Steps for descending from the Walks above. And at the upper part of the *Green Slopes* there are abundance of little Pipes of Water, about a Foot distance one from the other. Each of them hath a Copper Head, wherein there are four small holes, through which the Water is made to play, in order to Water the *Slopes*, and to preserve them always *Green*. In the Summer Evenings they are made frequently to rain a small Shower for the End aforesaid.

In the low Walk below the Green Slopes, at every four Yards distance, there are white Stones, each of them above a Foot and a half square, on every one of which there are *Urns*, and noble *Flowerpots* placed, or to be placed, as on Bases: And some of them have Representations of divers *Ancient* and *Modern Curiosities* carved upon them.

And all along the Wall of the *Lower Garden*, whither that which separates the first Terras-Walk from the *King's* and *Queens Garden*, or those that separate the higher Terras-Walks from the two *Wildernesses*, those Walls have such white square Stones near about the same distance from one another, and for the same purpose.

On the top of the said green *Slopes*, there do grow many *Pyramidal Juniper-Trees*, with other curious Shrubs intermixed among them. The *Slope* from the first Terras-Walk to the low Walk at bottom, is about eleven Foot; but the Slopes from the side Terras-Walks, to the said low Wall, have a descent of about 15 Foot, these being raised higher than the former Walk, on the account of the *Cascades* before-mentioned.

When we have descended into the *Garden* by the foresaid 18 Stone-steps, we do enter upon a broad Gravel Walk, into which advancing 45 Paces from the Steps, we come to a Noble Fountain, in the middle of whose *Basin* is a Marble Statue of *Venus* at full length, and another of *Cupid* under her left Hand, he holding a gilded Bow. This Statue is supported on a small *Whale* for its *Pedestal*, with four great gilded *Tritons* below it, a large gilded *Shell* being between each of the *Tritons*, and each *Triton* blowing in a large *Trumpet* in one Hand, their other Hand being disposed in different Postures. At the end of each *Trumpet* the Water runs out in a broad Sheet, incircling a great part of the broad end of the *Trumpet*. Also about the *Tritons* there were many gilded Rushes, and Water-lilly Flowers, which do all contribute to the Ornament of this *Magnificent Fountain*. On the right and left of this *Statue*, within the

same

same *Basin*, as also before and behind the *Statue*, there are four Gilded *Swans*, which do spout the Water in broad Sheets towards the *Statue*; and all the *Swans* are raised a little above the Water. The *Basin* is bordered with a blue Stone about 16 Inches breadth. It has four Angles, but on the four sides where the *Swans* are placed, it has a circumflexion or semicircular cut into the Walks, in form of four *Half-Moons*.

On either side of this *Broad Walk*, next to the Parterres, both before we come to the foresaid Fountain, and also on the sides of the Walk beyond the Fountain, there are *Spouts* at proper distances in a distinct *Canal*; and there are *six Spouts* in each of them, which do throw up the Water about a Yard, tho' of late those Spouts are now always stopt, to avoid the inconvenience of the Waters being blown on the Walk, or on the Parterres. These *Canals* are walled with Free-stone, and bordered with the same three Inches breadth. They are each of them about 80 Foot long, and a Foot and a half broad, but in those parts where the *Spouts* are placed, the *Canals* are widened unto three foot and a half square every way, in order to avoid the Winds blowing the Water either on the Walk, or Parterres. These *Canals* are paved after the *Mosaick* manner, with Pebbles of a dark colour, but the Figures that are made by the Pebbles, and which run along the middle of the *Canals*, and especially about the *Spouts*, are made in a long sort of Pebbles, pure white and black, of the Diamond-cut.

If we advance still forwards beyond the *Fountain* of *Venus* in the same Walk, we behold another Noble *Fountain*, in the middle of whose Basin is a young naked *Hercules* of Marble, arising as from his Cradle, also of Marble; the *Hercules* squeezing a green *Serpent* in each hand, and both the *Serpents* spirting the Water about two Yards above the Basin. On the right and left of the *Hercules*, at a little distance, within the same Basin, there are placed two *Dragons*, each spirting seven several *Jette*'s towards the *Hercules*. The Basin of this Fountain is likewise bordered with a broad blue Stone, 16 Inches breadth; and paved with a Stone that is about a foot square.

Turning out of the aforesaid Walk, from the Fountain of *Venus*, into a Cross-walk on the right, we meet with a *Fountain* in the middle, wherein is erected a *Celestial Globe*, placed on a Marble Pedestal, between which *Pedestal* and the *Globe* there are four naked *Boys* in Marble, incircling one another in their Arms. About the *Globe* the 12 *Signs* of the *Zodiack* are curiously painted, the *Stars* Gilded, and out of abundance of the *Stars* there do spout out *Jettes* on all sides of the *Globe*.

Passing beyond this *Globe*, we behold at the end of the Walk a most Noble *Cascade*, a Fabrick of wrought Stone, reaching from the Terras-Walk above, down to the Gravel-Walk below. The Water here falls out of the Mouth of a great *Head* at the top of the Structure (a round carved covered Basin being placed above the *Head*) into three great Semi-oval carved Basins, one below the other, each of them being two Yards in front, besides the allowance of above two foot more on both

[10]

sides of the two lowermost of those three Basins, which two Foot do serve for conveying the Water that is to make the lesser Sheets, which will be presently mentioned. On both sides of the uppermost of those three Semi-oval Basins there is placed a *Pine-apple* in Stone, by way of Ornamant; and on both sides of the second of those Basins, is erected a round scollopt Basin of two Foot diameter, that has a Spout in the middle, which throws up the Water about two Foot. From three parts of those round scollopt Basins, as well as from the whole front of the three great Semi-oval Basins, the Water does fall into the uppermost of six lesser Semi-oval Basins placed on each side. These lesser Basins are about a Yard in front, besides allowance of about two more for the forming of the smaller Falls of Water that are now to be mentioned. On each side of the six lesser Basions, both on the right and left of the Structure, there are made little Sheets of Water one below another in six Descents, contiguous to those made from the foresaid lesser Basins. But at the bottom of this Fabrick, between the Falls on both sides, there is an excellent Statue of *Narcissus* at length in Marble, standing upright, but looking a little downward into the Water in the common Basin, or Receiver below; and holding a Hunting-Horn in one Hand, whilst he draws up the other by way of Admiration, at the beholding of his own Reflection in the Water.

Again, turning from the *Fountain of Venus* on the left Hand the same distance in this Cross-Walk, as we did before from thence on the right to come to the *Celestial Globe*; there is, I say, on the left such another Noble Fountain, in the middle of which is erected a *Terrestrial Globe*. On this *Globe*, *Europe*, *Asia*, *Africa* and *America*, the four parts of the World, are exactly painted, and out of the several parts of it there do spring a great number of Spouts, which throw up the Water from all parts round it, as in the former *Globe*. This is likewise placed on a high Pedestal, round which there are four naked *Boys* in *Marble*, the first with a *Crown* on his Head, the second with a *Turbant*, the third a *Negro* in his short frizled Hair, and the fourth with long Hair hanging down his Back: The four Boys representing the Inhabitants of the four parts of the Earth.

At the end of this Walk, beyond this *Globe*, and on the slope of the opposite Terras-Walk, there is such another admirable *Cascade* as was just now described. Only in the middle of this *Cascade* there is a Marble Statue of *Galatea* sitting with a *Lute* in her Hand, at the bottom of the Fabrick, where *Narcissus* was placed in the former *Cascade*.

All along the middle of this Cross-Walk, between the Fountain of *Venus* and each of the *Globes*, as also between the *Globes* and the *Cascades* now described, there are little *Canals* without any *Jette's* in them, of the same length and make with the others that were placed on the sides of the first Walk.

This first Partition of the *Garden*, that contains all the aforesaid *Fountains* and *Cascades*, does likewise contain eight several *Parterres*, all

the

the *Quarters* being separated by Gravel-Walks on every side. The four inmost *Parterres* do consist of divers Figures in *Box*, encompassed with Beds of Flowers, and in those Beds there are intermixed many *Juniper-Trees* growing in Pyramidal Forms about round and high Staves painted Green. But the four *outmost Parterres* do consist of *Green Plots*, that have *Statues* placed upon high Pedestals in the middle of every one of them, and have Beds of Flowers a little interspersed among the *Green Plots*, besides other Beds of Flowers on all the outsides of those *Parterres*, next to the Gravel-Walks. The *Statues* in the middle of those *Green Quarters*, are excellently cut in Marble; they are of *Apollo* and *Pomona* on one side of the Garden, and of *Bacchus* and *Flora* on the other side, standing upright on the foresaid *Pedestals*.

The *Beds* and *Parterres* of this and the other *Gardens*, are not only adorned with *Pyramids of Juniper and Box*, and with Shrubs of *Marshmallows* of all colours, but contain variety of Flowers, which successively blow according to the Seasons of the Year. In the Spring there is a variety of the finest *Tulips, Hyacinths, Ranunculi, Anemone, Auricula ursi, Narcissus, Junci*, &c. In the Summer there are double *Poppies* of all colours, *Gilliflowers, Larks-heels*, &c. In the Autumn, the *Sun-Flower, Indian Cresses*, the *Pass-Rose* or *Stock-Rose, Marygolds*, &c. On the Walls of these Gardens do grow great variety of most excellent Fruit, as the best *Peaches, Apricocks, Cherries, Pears, Figs, Plums, Muscat Grapes* of all sorts; and their Props are every where painted Green.

At four Yards distance from the before-mentioned *Fountain* of *Hercules*, we advance forwards unto two broad Stone-steps, 13 Foot and a half in front; on both sides of which Steps there are *Stone-Rails* near five foot high, and on each side of the *Rails* are *Pilasters* of *Stone*, which are raised a Foot higher than the Rails. On the two *Pilasters* next to the Steps, are placed two Beautiful *Sphinxes*, with their Riddle express'd or carved; and on the two others are seen two *Wolfs* in Stone, each of them giving suck to a *Romulus* and *Remus*. From those *Pilasters* and *Rails* there is continued the whole breadth of the Garden a *Brick-Wall*, that is above four foot high, wherein there are also divers Pillars of Brick, faced with Free-stone, for the placing of Flowerpots.

CHAP. III.

Of the Second Part of the Great Garden, called the Upper Garden; together with the Middle Walk, and Canals, which do divide this Garden into the two Parts.

WHEN we are up the two Stone-steps now mentioned, we pass over a Canal into the *Middle Cross-Walk*, that divides this Garden, and is remarkable for its double row of tall Oaks on both sides of it. This Walk is eighteen yards broad from the two Stone-steps, and Rails, unto the Bridge over which we are to pass the second Canal, in

order

order to go into the Upper Garden. The *first Canal* is five foot broad, the second is 14 Foot. They run from West to East, and are supplied from *Cascades* that are made at the West-end of the foresaid Walk, which has Iron-rails fastned in Free-stone, that is half a Foot above the Brick-Wall, and that hath also divers Stone-Pilasters, ten Inches broad, and as high as the Iron-rails. Between those Rails there is a Gate of wrought Iron, through which we are to pass into the *Gardens* near the *Old Hoof.*

From a Marble *Head* placed in this Wall over the *Canals*, there is on each side a double fall of Water into two Stone-Basins, that are one below the other. The uppermost Basin is about a yard in front, and the lowermost a yard and a half.

About the *Bridge* of the *second Canal*, there is a *Stonework*, that is extended both East and West from the Bridge about 15 foot. At both ends of this Stone-work, which crosses the *Canal*, a *Fountain* rises in the middle of the Cross-wall, and by the declivity of a Basin both ways forms a sheet of Water both East and West, and also the same on both sides of the Bridge. Moreover, out of the Walls that are on both sides of this *Canal*, and also on each side of the *Bridge*, there are other falls of Water from *Stone-Basins*, besides some others in other parts of the *Canal*, made by raising the Water, or stopping its passage, to a certain heighth. These *Canals* are all along bordered with green Turf, and have a green Slope reaching from the border down to the Water.

Advancing forwards from the *second Canal* about 100 Paces, in a very broad Gravel-walk, we come to a most *Remarkable Fountain*, of a vast Circumference. The *Basin* of it is *Octangular*, and there are 16 Paces distance between each of the eight Angles. In the whole, it is a 128 Paces round. 'Tis bordered with a broad raised Stone-work, and paved with Pebbles, like many of the other Fountains, in divers sorts of uniform Figures. In the middle of this *Great Basin* there is a *Spout* that throws up the Water 44, or 45 foot high perpendicular. And round about this *Spout* there are placed two ranks of other *Spouts*, each of the ranks containing 16, which do all at a small distance encompass that High one in the middle. The inmost of these two ranks do throw up the Water 12 foot high, and the outmost rank six foot. This Noble Fountain containing no less than 33 *Spouts*, does make an agreeable shower of them together, and must abundantly please and divert the most curious Spectator. The Water of that *Spout* which throws it up so many foot high, is brought from a *Hill* two Leagues distant from *Lou*, and called *Asselt*. But the 16 *Spouts* which do immediately encompass that High Spout, are brought from another Source, called *Orden*, about a League off. And the rest of them are supplied from the *Viver.*

A little beyond this Great Fountain, in the same Walk, we descend by three wide Stone-steps to another admirable Fountain, in the middle of which there are 4 naked *Boys* in Marble, with 4 *Beasts* between them, those *Boys* and *Beasts* representing the *four parts of the World*. Over the *Boys Heads* there are four gilded *scollop Shells*, and over the inmost part of
those

those Shells a gilded *Basin inverted*. Out of the middle of this Basin the Water rises in form of a *Peacock's Tale* spread out at length, about a foot and a half above the *inverted Basin*. This Fountain hath its Basin bordered with Free-stone, sixteen inches broad, and its Stone-work raised three or four inches. From the said Border to the bottom of the Basin, there is rough Rockwork of divers Colours. But the bottom it self is bordered with White Marble ten inches round, and the rest of the bottom is paved with dark Pebble, among which there are also intermixed Marble Stones in divers Figures.

As we do ascend from this Fountain forwards, we meet with a Fall of Water from *one semioval Stone Basin*, extended four foot and a half in front, and placed between three Stone Steps on each side of it. At the four Corners of those Steps, Bases are raised for the placing of Flower-pots. And round this Fountain there is a Green Slope equal to the heighth of the Steps, by which we descend to, or ascend from the aforesaid *Fountain*. Farthermore, between those Steps and the Border of the Basin to this Fountain, there is a round Gravel Walk above four yards broad.

Going ten Paces forwards beyond the former *Cascade*, we come to another, where the Water falls from *Three Stone Basins*, one below another; whereof the uppermost is about three foot in front, that in the middle four foot and a half, and the lowermost five foot, besides a farther extension of these Basins on both sides, for the making of lesser Sheets of Water of eleven inches each in front, which are likewise one below another in three descents. Here is also an ascent of five Stone Steps on both sides of the Water, with four Bases at the four Corners of those Steps, for the placing of Flower-pots.

So soon as we are up these Steps, we do presently turn on the right and left of the Walk into *Semicircular Galleries* or *Porticoes*, below which there are two Green *Slopes*, one below the other; and between those *Slopes* there are Flower-pots disposed the whole length of them. Each of these *Galleries* is forty paces long, and about six yards broad; and each of them is supported by *twenty Pillars*. They are covered with *Lead* to shelter from the Rain, and have White Ballisters four foot high upon the *Leads*, to which there is an ascent by Stairs behind the *Galleries*. On the Wall within the *Galleries*, there are drawn the Gods and Goddesses at length in *Fresco*, thirteen of them in each *Gallery*. They are paved with White and Red Brick. At the farther end of them there is a descent of seven Steps into the Garden.

Beyond these *Galleries* the former Walk continues between Kitchen Gardens on our right and left, but we cannot see them by reason of a Hedge of *Dutch* Elm five yards high. At the farther end of this Walk Northwards, we come to another *Cascade* and *Fountain*. The *Cascade* is from one plain, long Basin, about eight foot in front. On both sides of it we do ascend by three Stone Steps that are five yards in length, unto another *Fountain*, that has no *Spout* in it. The Basin of it is oval, and but seven foot in length. On both sides of this *Fountain* there are *Seats*, covered above, painted behind in *Fresco*, and paved below with *white Marble*. The open space about this *Fountain*, and between the *Seats*, is paved with a Black, White, and Yellowish Pebble, set in divers Figures.

And here going up two Stone-steps more, that are extended the whole breadth of the Walk, we are stopt from going farther by large Iron Balusters, and a *Canal* beyond them. In the Canal below, there is another *Fountain* in the midst of *Garlands*, made of Shells, Petrified Earths, or spungy Stones, from the top of which the Water does fall on three rows, or Garlands of the same substances, placed one below another. Lastly, on both sides of this *Fountain* there are other Falls of Water to be seen below.

Nor is our View here limited, though our Passage be; for looking on still forwards, we carry our Prospect between Trees, unto a *high Pyramid*, erected in the *Heath*, about half a Mile's distance from the end of the *Garden*.

In this *Second Division* of the *Garden* there are twelve *Parterres*, with Gravel-walks between them all. The six inmost *Quarters* adjoining, three of a side, to the middle Broad-walk, through which we passed, do consist of divers Figures in green, encompassed with Beds of Flowers, in the which there are divers Juniper Trees growing up Pyramidal about green round Staves, and placed at convenient distances. The six outermost of these *Quarters*, next to the Garden-wall on both sides, are all plain green.

From the low Wall at the bottom of the first Terras-walk, unto the Stone Rails or Steps in the *Lower Garden* on the South-side of the middle Cross-walk, it is about a hundred and twelve Paces. And from the Steps of the side Terras-walk on the right, unto the opposite Steps of the other Terras-walk on the left, it is two hundred and twenty Paces.

Beyond the aforesaid Cross-walk, from thence unto the *Galleries*, it is a hundred and forty Paces; and thence to the *Iron Bars* at the farther end, about a hundred Paces more.

CHAP.

CHAP. IV.

Of the King's Garden, *and another Westward of it;* *called the* Labyrinth.

ON the West-side of the *Palace*, under His *Majesty's* Apartments, there is a Garden called the *King's Garden*; which consists of two Divisions. The one has three *Parterres*, and a *Fountain* near the middle of them. The other is a large *Bowling-green*. The three Parterres do consist of Beds of Flowers, bordered with Box in divers Figures, with Pyramids of Juniper, or Box, in many parts of them. The *Fountain* is bordered with white Marble, thirteen Inches broad: In the middle of this *Fountain* there is a gilded *Triton*, holding under his left Arm a gilded *Dolphin*, out of whose Mouth springs a *Jette*, that throws up the Water about six foot high. On the *border* of this *Fountain* there are placed at convenient distances eight gilded *Sea-Dragons*, every one spirting the Water upon the *Triton* in the middle.

The *Bowling-green* lies on the South-side of this Garden, and has the *King Stables* adjoining on two sides of it.

At the West-end of the Gravel-walk, that is between the *King's Garden* and the *Bowling-green*, we do pass through a Gate of Iron Rails, partly gilded, and partly painted Blew, into another Garden, called the *Labyrinth*, or Wilderness.

When we have here cross'd a Gravel-walk, a Hedge, and a Green-walk, we come to an ascent of three Stone-steps, on both sides of which there is a Stone Fabrick with Ballisters in the middle, and four wrought Flowerpots covered, one on each side of the Ballisters. From the Stone-work on each side of the Steps, the Water falls from three Marble Heads into a common Basin bordered and walled with Stone; in each of these Basins there are two *Spouts* which do throw up the Water six foot high.

Advancing Westward from the said Steps about thirty six Paces, we come to a *Fountain*, in the middle of which there are *four Sea-Cupids* in Stone, sitting on *four Dolphins*. Between the *Cupids* there rises a *Spout* out of a *Serpent's Head*, that throws up the Water about five foot, and out of every Nostril of the four *Dolphins* there do run other little *Spouts*. The Border of the Basin of this Fountain is of raised Stone-work; and it is paved with white Pebbles, but towards the Angles (the Basin being octangular) there are Figures of large Flowerdeluces in a dark Pebble.

At this *Fountain* there are *eight* several *Walks* to be seen, between Hedges of an equal heighth, all the Hedges being between seven and

and eight foot high. Of these eight Walks four are Green, and the four others are of Earth without Turf, and ungravelled. The Green Walks are placed between the others. At the end of all these Walks there are to be seen *Statues*, or *Paintings*, and Westward from the Fountain, besides a large piece of Painting, there is a *Fountain* with two *Spouts*, and a fall of Water out of a *Head* placed below the *Painting*.

North and South from this Fountain, at forty Paces distance, we come unto other Fountains. In the middle of that Northwards, there are two *little Boys* of Stone, with an *Otter* between them, out of whose mouth there rises a *Jette*, six foot high. It is bordered with rough Rockwork of divers colours, with some large *Conchæ*, or Shells intermixed: The bottom of the Basin is paved with white and brown Pebbles in different Figures.

At the same distance from the Fountain of the *Sea-Cupids* Southward, there is another Fountain, in the middle of which there is a *naked Boy* in Stone, holding a scollopt Shell in his hand, through which there rises another *Jetee* like to the last now mentioned; and below this *Boy* there is a *Satyr* in Stone. The Basin of this is bordered, like the other, with rough Stones and Shells, and the Paving is with Pebbles, after the *Mosaick* manner.

Beyond these three Fountains, North and South, the Walk is continued to some distance; and from all those Fountains there are other Walks also to the East and West.

And besides these Walks now mentioned, there are other Walks and Turnings between the Hedges, into which when we have gone a little way, we are obliged to return into some of the former Walks by the way we entered. Lastly, The Ground that is between these Hedges, Walks, and Turnings, is all planted with *Fruit-trees* of divers kinds.

CHAP. V.

Of the Queen's Garden, *and another Private Garden, or* Labyrinth *beyond it,* Eastward.

ON the East-side of the *Palace*, there is a Garden that is called the *Queen's Garden*, being under the *Apartments* appointed for her *Majesty*, as the *King's Garden* before described was on the *King's* side. Both of them are of the same dimensions.

This Garden is divided into two Parts; whereof the one, being next to the *Great Garden*, consists of three *Parterres* of Flowers, bordered with Box, and having Pyramidal Juniper Trees in divers parts

of

of them. The *Parterres* are on all sides encompassed with Gravel-walks; and on the Walls here are divers sort of Fruit-trees, Grapes, &c. besides Paintings of *Floras*, &c. in some places.

In the middle of the Parterres is a Fountain of *Arion* gilded, playing on a *Lute*, and riding on a gilded *Dolphin*, out of whose Nostrils there do rise two *Spouts* five or six foot high. The Basin is bordered with white Marble, thirteen Inches broad. On the border are placed at convenient distances eight gilded *Sea-Horses*, every one making a *Jette* out of each Nostril. The Basin is paved with a square Stone, about a foot broad. On both sides of this Fountain are Seats painted green, next to the Parterres.

The other Part of this Garden consists of divers Gravel-walks within *Arbors*, the whole length and breadth of it, and has five *Fountains* in the middle of all the *Arbors*. Into the middle of the first *Arbor-walk* there is an ascent of four Steps, besides a like ascent of Steps at both ends of the same Walk, without the *Arbors*; or between them and the Garden Walls. Between those three pair of Steps, there is a green Slope the height of the Steps, and at the top of the Slope there are long Beds of Flowers, with Juniper Trees intermixed. And at the corners of all the Steps there are Flower-pots.

The first Arbor-walk that runs from West to East, and is next to the Garden now described, hath eight open Spaces or Windows, towards the *Parterres*, besides eight other such Windows on the inside, whereas the other three Sides or Arbor-walks have their Windows only on the inside of the Walk. These Windows are five foot and a half long, and near upon the same heigth; and they are square at bottom, and convex at top. The four long *Arbor-walks*, on the four sides of this Part of the *Queen's Garden*, are each above threscore Paces long, and twelve foot and a half wide. At the four corners, or ends of these Walks, there is placed a *Cupid* above the Seat, and from those Seats we can see through Windows cut in the inward *Arbors*, diametrically cross this Part of the Garden, three of the five Fountains, that are presently to be described.

Besides the four Gravel-walks within the Arbors, and three other Gravel-walks without the Arbors, next to the Garden-wall; there are other Walks within Arbors that are not gravelled, the which do wind and turn in uniform Figures from the middle of one of the side Arbor-walks to the middle of another. And between these three are Parterres with Fountains in them.

In the middle of all the *Arbors* there is a *Fountain* with a large gilded *Triton*, sitting on a Rock of Stones and Shells, and blowing through a gilded *Horn* a *Spout* about eight foot high. The *Basin* is border'd with rough Rockwork. It is paved with Pebbles, and white Marble set among them, cut in oval, or Diamond forms. From the

middle

middle of the four long Arbor-walks unto this Fountain there are four direct Walks, and between these Walks there are four little Gardens, or Parterres, separated from the said Gravel-walks by Hedges of *Dutch Elm*, about four foot high.

In the middle of each of these four little Gardens, there is a distinct Fountain, and in each of the Fountains there is placed a gilded *Triton*, sitting on a gilded *Sea-Horse*, or on a *Sea-Goat*, all upon Rockwork, like that in the middle Fountain; and the Basins of these are paved like the former. But these *four Tritons* and Basins are less in proportion than that in the middle Fountain. One of these four *Tritons* holds a *Cup* in his Right hand, through which there rises a *Jette* six or seven foot. The second holds a *Trident* in his hand, and through the three Spikes of the *Trident* are made three Dards or Spouts. The third holds a *Fish*, and makes a *Spout* through the Mouth of the *Fish*. And the fourth blows another through a twined *Trumpet*. All the *Spouts* in these four Fountains do rise much about the same heigth. And besides these, the *Sea-horses* on which the four *Tritons* do ride, do all make a little sheet of water from their Tongues.

About the first and largest of these five *Tritons*, placed in the middle of those other four Fountains, and the Arbors, there are eight semicircular *Seats*, covered behind and over head Arbor-like; the *Seats* and Prop-work, as also the Prop-work of all the Arbors being painted green. Every one of these *Seats* is above eight foot wide, and ten foot high. And between the four Gravel-walks, which come to this Fountain from the middle of the four Side-Arbor walks, there are two of these eight Seats, as also between every two Seats there is an entrance five foot wide into the Parterres of one of the four lesser Fountains.

All along these Gravel-walks, and round the middle Fountain, there are placed Orange-trees, and Lemmon-trees in portable Wooden-frames, and Flower-pots about them.

In a corner of the *Queen's Garden*, next to the Terras-walk of the *Great Garden*, and under one corner of the *Palace*, there is a fine *Grotto*, consisting of the Roots of Trees, Flints, and Shells, disposed in a rough *Grotesco* manner, and in one corner of this *Grotto* there is an *Aviary*.

The Room for the *Grotto* is paved with Black and White *Marble*, there being two Fountains in it overagainst one another, and they are raised Arch-wise from the bottom to the top of the Room, the border round the Fountains being raised above a foot from the floor, in order to hinder the Water from wetting the Room. The sides are embellished with divers sorts of Shells, and all parts of the Windows beautified with the same, in divers Figures. There are three Gates or Passages into this Room, one from the *Queen's Garden*,

another

another from the *Great Garden*, under the Terras-walk, the third goes into a little Room, where a Couch is placed for Repose, and thence we go into another Room adorned all over with abundance of *Porceline*, or *China*.

The *Aviary* is exposed to the open Air, but incompassed with a small Grate, to confine the Birds; and there is a place in the corner of the *Grotto* for the Birds to retreat into, from the Rain, or Weather.

On the Eastside of the *Queen's Garden*, there is another Garden for retirement, with Walks, and Hedges of Witch-Elm, about eight foot high; into which we do pass out of the former through a Gate of wrought Iron, painted Blew and Gilt. Turning in it Northwards in the second Walk, we come to a Noble *Fountain*, unto which we descend by six Steps; but in the middle of these Steps there is a small fall of Water in six descents from a *Fountain* at the top of the Steps; and from thence the Water runs in a small channel cross the Walk that encompasses the Fountain which I am going to describe.

This *Fountain* is oblong, or of an Oval figure; its *diameter* is in length twenty Paces, and it is about ten Paces wide. In the middle of this *Basin* there is a round Rock, of rough Stones, Shells, and Forgecinders, about a yard above the Water. Out of this *Rockwork* there springs a *Jette* about five yards high, from the middle of it; and from the other parts round about this *Rock* there do rise abundance of other *Spouts*. This *Fountain* is bordered with green Turf, on the Slope of which Border there are placed at due distances six *scollopt Shells* of wrought Stone. Into all these *Shells* there is a fall of Water from the mouth of a wrought *Head*, joined to the *Shell* in one and the same Stone; and from four parts of each *Shell* the Water falls into the Basin of the Fountain, which is not paved at all, the bottom being only of Earth, as the Border of it and the Slope were of Turf.

Round this *Fountain*, next to the Hedge, and directly behind the foresaid *six Shells*, there are *six Statues* in Stone, or so many little *Cupids* standing upon high Pedestals of wrought Stone; and at the bottom of each Pedestal there is a fall of Water into a small square Stone-basin, from whence the Water runs under the Walk into one of the *Heads* and *Shells* that were before mentioned to be placed on the Slope below the Border. The first of these *Cupids* is drinking out of a *Stone-cup* held in one hand, and has a *bunch of Grapes* in the other. The second holds a *Tulip* in his right hand. The third is reading in a *Book*, through a pair of Spectacles, held near the Book. The fourth has a Play-thing in his hand. The fifth has a *Snake*, which he squeezes hard in his Arms. And the sixth leans upon a *Spade*. Also round about this Fountain there are placed fifty *Orange-trees* in Frames.

Going

[18]

Going still Northwards about thirty Paces from this Fountain, we come at the end of this Walk to a Statue of *Venus* at length, a little stooping, and holding *Cupid* by both hands. The *Venus* is placed on a Stone Pedestal, and out of a wrought Head at the bottom of the Pedestal, there is a fall of Water into a small Stone-basin.

A little Eastward of this Statue of *Venus*, there is another *Fountain* in a square Stone-basin. In the middle of it there is a small fall of Water from a round Stone-basin, whence the Water does fall equally all round in one sheet. And besides another *Cascade* that is here made out of a *Head* into a large Basin, there are five other falls of Water from out of the Walls of this Fountain, each of them about a foot in breadth.

CHAP. VI.

Of the Voliere, *or* Fowl-Garden.

AT the West-end of the *Middle Walk* that divides the *Great Garden* into *two Parts*, we pass through a *Gate* of wrought Iron, into a Walk between high Trees, that goes Southward into the first *Labyrinth*, described in the Fourth Chapter, and Northwards as far as the *Heath*, that is beyond all the *Gardens*.

At this Garden-gate, we behold the *Old Hoof* directly before us Westward, but are separated from it by two *Moats*, between which there are five rows of *Lime-trees* ; on the South of which the *Labyrinth* is seated, and on the North the *Fowl Garden*, that is now to be described.

Advancing from the foresaid Gate fifty paces North-wards, we turn to the Gate of the *Fowl Garden* on our left, to which we pass on a Bridge over the Moat. This Gate is likewise of wrought Iron, painted Blew and Gilt. Going from this Gate two and twenty paces, we descend by three Steps to a Noble *Fountain* and *Cascade*, round which *Fountain* from the bottom of the Steps to the Border of its Basin there is a Walk twelve foot and a half broad, into which Walk there are four descents by three Steps, four opposite ways: And between the one and the other row of Steps there is a Green Slope round the Fountain.

The *Basin* of this *Fountain* is oblong, or oval, and of a great circumference, the *Diameter* at least forty paces in length, and about twenty four paces in breadth. It is designed for the use of divers sorts of *Fowl* ; and there are *Houses* built on the two sides of this Garden, for sheltering the *Fowl*. In the middle of this *Fountain* there is a *Jette*, that throws up the Water about twenty foot ; and
below

below the *Jette* there is a triple *Cafcade*, made from three round Bafins, whereof the uppermoft appears to make a fheet about a foot in depth, the middle-one near about two foot, and the lowermoft four foot. Between thefe three Bafins the fpaces or intervals are filled all round with *Shells*, &c. the which *Shells* are feen round them through the Sheets of Water that fall from the said *Bafins*.

On the North and South-fide of this Fountain, fix yards from one of the defcents by three Steps, there are two *Summer Houfes*, the one oppofite to the other. They are within painted in *frefco* and *bronze*, and have *Cupola*'s over them, painted Blew and Gilded. Into thefe *Houfes* we enter by folding Doors, which confift of two foot Wainfcot from the bottom, the reft in broad Glafs up to the *Cupola*. Each of thefe *Houfes* hath four Shafh-windows, befides the Doors, and hath on each fide of them, contiguous to the middlemoft and largeft Windows, an *Aviary*, wherein are kept curious Foreign, or Singing Birds. When the Shafh-windows next to the *Aviaries* are opened, there is ftill a Wire-grate remaining, to hinder the Birds from flying out of their *Aviaries* into the *Summer-houfes*. Thefe Houfes are paved with white and red Marble, cut into curious Figures, but they are bordered all round with black Marble, of half a foot breadth, over which Border there is alfo a Ledge of white Marble, between the black, and the Wainfcot.

The *Aviaries* that adjoin to the *Summer-houfes*, are likewife covered with leffer *Cupola*'s of Lead, painted Blew and gilded; but the large *Cupola* in the middle has a round Glafs-window, and another little *Cupola* in the middle has a round Glafs-window, and another little *Cupola* above the Window, and on the top of the higheft *Cupola* in each Houfe there is a Gilded Pine-apple placed on a Gilded Bafis. Thefe *Aviaries* have on three fides Grates of Wire, which do reach from the *Cupola* above, to a Stone-wall about two foot high at bottom. The two outmoft Side-grates have wooden Shutters without them, and thofe Shutters an oval Glafs-window in them towards the top. In the middle of the *Aviaries* there is a *Jette*, whofe Water falls into a little fhallow leaden Bafin, near a yard fquare. Behind thefe *Aviaries* there are other leffer ones, open above, and on one fide, for the receiving fome particular Birds, that muft be more in the open Air, or that muft be kept alone by themfelves.

And befides thefe *Aviaries*, there are in two corners of this Garden, on the Northweft, and Southeaft, two other *Houfes* in three divifions, for Ducks, Pigeons, Poultrey, &c. with holes on both fides at the bottom for the Fowl to enter. The middle part of thefe Houfes is now ufed for tame Pigeons, and has a large Wire-grate towards the Air, and a Spout in the middle, that falls into a fhallow round Leaden Bafin of about two foot diameter.

Round the uppermost Walk that encompasses this Fountain, there are high Stakes joined together, five yards above this Walk, being a prop for the Hedges to grow on, that are now of that height, according to the manner that is frequently used in the *Low Countries*. In four places of this Hedge there are also semicircular *Arbors*, of the height of the Hedge, with Seats at convenient distances from the Summer-houses.

Between this Hedge and the Wall of this Garden there are some plain *Parterres* bordered with Box, and in other places Ever-Greens set here and here.

CHAP. VII.

Of the Park, *and its* Fountains, Long Canal, Cascade, *&c. together with the* Viver, *that supplies the* Fountains *and* Cascades *with Water; as also a description of six other* Vivers, *or* Fish-ponds.

THE *Park* is a great space of Ground containing many Long Green *Walks, Groves, Nurseries, Fountains, Canals, Cascades,* the *Viver*, and divers Corn-fields, within the Pales. So that when His *Majesty* is pleased to take diversion at home, there is not wanting Game for *Shooting, Setting,* &c.

As we go from the *Fowl-Garden* Westwards, we do leave the *Old Hoof* on the left hand, and at the West-end of this Garden we come to a large Wire-grate, of the bigness of a large Gate, on both sides of which Grate we pass through Doors into the *Park*, and first to a *Long Canal*, in the which there are no less than a hundred and eight *Spouts*, half on one side, and the other half on t'other side of the *Canal*. They throw the Water above four foot high, and the Water of every *Spout* is made to fall on the contrary side of the *Canal*. This *Canal* is about six foot broad, and the distance between every one of the *Spouts* is five foot, so as that between every two on the same side there are ten foot distance. At the beginning and end of the *Canal*, there are placed two *Spouts* falling the one upon the place of the other; but all the rest do fall on the contrary side, and distant from the opposite Spouts, the whole length of the *Canal*. All these *Spouts* do fall into the figure of an Arch.

This *Canal* reaches from the Gate of the *Fowl-Garden* already described, unto a *Great Cascade* that will be presently mentioned; it has Hedges on each side five yards high; and on the farther side of the Hedge South of the *Canal*, has a stately Grove of tall Trees, and Northwards of it has all along a Nursery of young ones. About

half

half way, the Walk on each side between the Hedge and the Border of the *Canal* is about five foot broad, but the other half way, next the *Cascade*, the Walk is widened unto fifteen foot on both sides. The *Canal* is Bordered with Green Turf, and has a Slope of the same from the Border down to the Water.

About the middle of this *Canal*, on the South-side, there is placed a Marble Statue of a *Flora* at length, on a high Stone Pedestal; and on each side of the *Flora* there is also a Head; the which Statue and Heads are seen as at the end of a long Green Walk North of the *Canal*, the which Walk is a hundred and seventy Paces, to go from the *Canal* unto the Fountain of *Faunus*, that will soon be described.

At the West-end of this *Long Canal*, we come to a most Noble Fabrick of wrought Stone, or to the *Cascade* of the *Fishers*, sometimes also called the Cypher Fountain. It is joined to the side of one of the Walks about the *Viver*; it has Ballisters at the top of the Fabrick, and joining to the Walk above; and there are covered Flowerpots upon the Ballisters. On each side of this *Cascade* there are two several ascents by Stone-steps. And first we come to four Steps, on the corners of which there are placed two little *Dragons*, out of whose mouths the Water falls into two scollopt Stone Basins at the bottom, under the *Dragons*. From these four Steps on both sides, we cross over other *Canals* by a Stone-bridge, and then come to eleven Stone-steps more. These *Canals* do serve to carry away good part of the Water that makes this *Cascade*, and the rest of it runs into the *Long Canal*, just now described.

In the middle of this *Cascade*, below the Ballisters, there are four little *Boys a fishing*, and drawing a *Nett* full of Fish; the four little *Boys* are of Stone, with leaden Net-work coloured like Stone, in their Arms; and through a great deal of this Net-work placed between the *Boys*, the Water falls into a large wrought *Basin*, and from this *Basin* the Water falls again in five several places between other Net-work. Two of these falls of Water from the said Basin are made into a Stone *Canal* below, that runs along the side of the Wall, under the Stone Bridges into the *Canals* on the North and South sides of the *Cascade*. The three other falls are thence made first upon Rockwork, and from thence into a common or general Basin that receives the Water aforesaid, besides what comes from the *Spouts*, and *Bell*, that will be presently mentioned.

Moreover, into the said *Canal* that runs along the side of the Wall of this *Cascade*, there are four other falls of Water, whereof the two outward are from two *Heads* of Stone, the two inward from two *Heads* of Marble, placed at due distances in the Wall aforesaid. The Water from the Heads of Stone falls directly into the *Canal*, but from the Heads of *Marble* it falls into Stone-basins, that are about a yard in front, and from them the sheet of Water falls into the said *Canal*. Besides, out of the lower Wall of this *Canal* there are two other falls out of two more *Heads* of *Marble* into two other *Stone*-basins of the same bigness with the former, and directly under those *Heads* of *Marble* and Basins, that were before mentioned to be placed in the upper Wall of the Canal, or the Side-wall of the *Cascade*. And from these two Basins the sheets of Water do fall into the general Basin at bottom.

In the middle of the common Basin there is a large inverted *Bell* of Water, near two yards high, and the *diameter* of its *basis* on the top seems to be much about two yards likewise. About this *Bell* there do arise twelve Spouts which throw up the Water about eight foot. On the North and South sides of the Basin wherein were the said *Great Bell*, and the twelve Spouts, there are other *lesser Bells* of Water inverted, on each side one. These do rise about a foot high, and the *diameter* of them at the top is much the same. The *common Basin* below the *Cascade* is bordered with a broad Stone of sixteen inches breadth, and walled with Rockwork ; and the whole space between the said Border, and the *Long Canal* before described, as well as to the Stone-stairs on either side of this *Cascade*, is taken up chiefly with little Stone-Canals of seven inches breadth, their Border but two inches. But in the intervals between those little *Canals* the space is paved with white and black Pebbles in divers Figures. From the two *lesser Bells* the Water does run along those little *Canals*, which, besides the flourish they do make on each side, do form the Letters *R. W. M. R.* And above those Letters the said small *Canals* are so disposed, as to form the representation of a *Crown*. Moreover, from among these Pebbles, with which all the intervals between the little *Canals* are paved, there are made to rise, when 'tis thought fit, by the turning of two *Cocks*, about fourscore the most minute Spouts that can be conceived. They are like a shower of small rain, artificially made in a certain order. One half of the fourscore is made to play by the turning of one *Cock*, and t'other half by turning the other. And these *Cocks* are turned in the Walk above the *Cascade*, or between it and the *Viver*. Every one of these little *Spouts* plays about a yard high, and the Pipe of every one of them is covered with a small Copper Cover, that has five little holes through which the Water does rise in five small branches, like to a very small shower of Rain. Some of the Covers of these Pipes are half an inch, others are three quarters of an inch diameter. But in short, they do make a very pleasant and agreeable sight, whenever they are made to play : And they are intended to divert the Spectators, by causing a small Rain unawares on those who shall advance within the compass of their reach.

I did before mention two pair of Stone-steps, the one of four, the other of eleven Steps on the North and South sides of this *Cascade*. From the two sides of the lowermost, or least pair of Steps, where

the

the little *Dragons* were said to be placed, there are continued from the Steps on one side to the Steps on the other side of the *Cascade*, all round this space (which was said to be paved with Pebbles, and to consist of the foresaid Stone *Canals*) two *circles* of *Stone* of fourteen inches breadth, which do serve instead of a *double Border* to the whole; the two *Borders* keeping the same distance from one another throughout, as the Steps do make in front, or breadth.

When we are up the second pair of Stairs of eleven Steps, we enter upon a Walk, that encompasses a large *Quadrangular Pond*, called the *Viver*, being the common Storehouse of the *Water* that supplies so many of these *Fountains*, *Cascades*, and *Canals*. The Walk on the four sides of the *Viver* is seven yards broad; it is a Gravelled Walk; and on the side next to the Water it is adorned with *Juniper-trees* two yards high, and six yards distance from one another; and on the other side of it has *Lime-trees* at the same distance, besides large round Bushes between the *Lime-trees*. The *Viver* is a hundred and forty paces long, and threescore and ten paces broad. It is bordered with green, and has a green *Slope* from the Border down to the Water.

At the West-end of the *Viver*, in the middle of the Walk, we do pass through another Gate, the Bars partly Gilt, and partly Blew, into a long shady *Grove*, usually called the *Queen's Grove*, wherein there are divers Walks, some near unto *Brooks* of a clear running Water, others at some distance from the *Brooks*, and all of them as solitary and retired, as can well be imagined. This Grove is of a good extent, and in the Summer-time very delightful.

And now before we end, let us return unto the East-gate of the *Fowl-Garden*, from whence we may enter North-west into a long Walk between high Trees, there being a *Grove* on each side beyond the rows of Trees. In this Walk, when we have gone about two hundred and twenty paces, and there cross'd another long green Walk, towards the middle of this Walk, where the *Groves* do end, we do at length come to the Fountain of *Faunus*, whose Basin is round, and about fifty seven foot *diameter*. In the middle of this *Fountain* there is erected the Statue of *Faunus* in Stone at length, with an *Infant* in his Arms, and a *Goat* at his Feet to suckle the *Infant*. This Statue of *Faunus* does lean upon a Stone *Pillar*, and stands upon a high *Pedestal* of a Blew Stone, placed in the midst of a Rock, consisting of many rough Stones, petrified Earth of divers colours, and large Shells here and there intermixed. From about this Rockwork there are made six double sheets of Water, whereof each double fall is over-against a several Walk. For from this *Fountain* there are six distinct *Walks*, one opposite to another. And round about it, between each of the *six Walks*, near the corners of the *Walks*, there are placed two *Statues* in half-length of the *Termini*, or Gods of Boundaries, twelve in all; some of which twelve *Statues* have the face

face of a *Man*, and some of a *Satyr*; and they are placed upon Pedestals two yards high. All these *Walks* are twenty two, or twenty four foot broad; they are green in the middle, and on each side of the Green they are plain Earth ungravelled, according to the *Dutch* custom, to about four foot and a half breadth on each side of the Green. The *Hedges* of all these *Walks* do consist of Trees both great and small, planted close together. Here are also other handsome *long-Walks* in the Park, that are not mentioned; besides *Brooks*, and *Fish-ponds* within the *Grove* on the sides of the *Long Canal*.

There is one thing more very remarkable in these many *Fountains* and *Cascades* that have been described; as that they are supplied with a natural conveyance of Water that does constantly run, and is not forc'd up with *Engines* into great *Cisterns*, where it must soon corrupt and stink, if not quickly discharged. Whence it comes to pass, that the famous *Water-works* at *Versailles* have in this regard a very great disadvantage and inconvenience, because they soon contract corruption, and after they are forc'd to play, are found to cause an *ill stench* in the *Gardens*. Whereas at *Loo* the Water is always sweet, and there is no need of Commands, or Preparations for a Day or two before, in order to make it run.

These *Gardens* in the whole are a Work of wonderful *Magnificence*, most worthy of so *Great* a *Monarch*; a Work of prodigious Expence, infinite Variety, and Curiosity; and after nine years labour by abundance of Workmen they were some years ago intirely finished, and brought to perfection in all respects.

I should here conclude this Description, if I did not judge it may be acceptable to give a short account of six *Vivers*, or Fish-ponds, which His *Majesty* has caused to be made in the *Heath*, beyond the *Gardens*. When I was at *Loo*, two years since, there were about two hundred Persons employed in the making the said *Vivers*, which are since finished. They are situated on the East-side of that Walk which is continued from the end of the *Upper Garden*, between *Lime-trees*, unto a *Pyramid* that is erected half a Mile off in the *Heath*.

The first of these *Vivers* is about twenty yards distant from the *Lime-trees*, and is eight hundred and forty foot, or two hundred and eighty yards in length. And it is two hundred and forty foot, or fourscore yards in breadth.

All the *six Vivers* do lye Eastward of one another, and the Water is conveyed from one to another, after the manner as in the *Fish-ponds* in *Hide-park*. To the first there is made a subterranean Passage, built of Brick, from the Canal that runs at the North-end of the *Great Garden*, by the which Passage the Water is brought into the first *Viver*, and from that let into the others.

The second *Viver* is in length six hundred and twelve foot, or two hundred and four yards; and it is two hundred and forty foot, or fourscore yards broad.

The

The third *Viver* is four hundred forty four foot, or a hundred forty eight yards long; and of the same breadth with the two former.

The fourth, fifth, and fixth *Vivers*, are all of the same length, that is, three hundred ninety six foot, or one hundred thirty two yards long; and they are all three of the same breadth, that is, four hundred forty four foot, or one hundred forty eight yards.

The length of the three first *Vivers* is extended *Northwards*, but that of the three latter is made *Eastward*; the situation of the Ground, wherein they are made, requiring this alteration. For on the North-side the *Heath* has a rising ascent, which makes this alteration of the dimensions necessary. Between the *Vivers* and this rising-ground there is room enough for receiving the Water that shall at any time be emptied out of them, in order to fill them with fresh Water.

They are not made above six foot deep, and the Earth that is dug out of them does serve to make the *Banks* round about them; the which *Banks* being raised three foot above the *Vivers*, does occasion that their depth is but three foot more. The *Banks* that surround all the *six Vivers* are twenty four foot broad, and on those *Banks* which so encompass them, there is made a pleasant Walk, adorned with *Willows* the whole circumference. But the *Banks* which serve to separate them from one another, are but eighteen foot broad. These *Vivers* are provided for the supplying different sorts of *Fish*; and are now finished by a Model of Monsieur *Marot*, a very ingenious Mathematician, who is the same Person that first *Designed* all these *Gardens* and *Fountains*; but the Orders relating to them were from time to time given by the Right Honourable the Earl of *Portland*; and his Lordship's Directions were punctually observed by Monsieur *des Marais*, His *Majesty's* Chief Architect, a Gentleman of great Endowments and Capacity.

A short Account of HOLLAND.

IN the foregoing Description I have given the Reader a moderate comprehension of those famous *Gardens*; the *finishing* of which so nobly, and with that great variety, is the more to be Admired, because it was done *during the late War*, when all things were at stake, and the event was feared so much by most Men. And although things were not indeed in that danger from the *French*, as the *Roman State* was, when *Hannibal* was at the Gates of *Rome*; yet it puts me in mind of a Brave Action of that Great People, who,

who, whilst *Hannibal* was just under their Walls with his Army, and some of the *Fields* whereon he was Incamped, happening to be then exposed to *Publick Sale*, were not destitute of Purchasers of that Magnanimity, who at that very time gave even the Market Price for an Estate then in possession of the Greatest and most Deadly Enemy that ever threatned that *Republick*, from the first *Founding* of the *City*.

And this is the more remarkable, because the *French King*, at the breaking out of this War, though his Coffers were then full of an inexhaustible Treasure, as 'twas thought; and though he had an Inclination to Magnificent Buildings beyond all his Predecessors, yet he immediately Ordered a *full stop* to be put to all his *Publick Works*: Well foreseeing what a terrible Storm he had brought upon his Kingdom, and with how *Great a General* he was like to contend. Insomuch that this *Grand Monarch*, who was often said to give *Peace* to *Europe*, out of a certain peculiar Generosity, when he had on a sudden snatcht away from his Neighbours one Province after another, and his *Slow Enemies* had begun to form their Forces; this *Monarch*, I say, was by the late long and Expensive *War*, by the firmness of the *Confederate Union*, and by the prospect of a *Peace* with the *Turks*, brought to such Fears and Apprehensions, that he *Purchased* a *Peace* with a strange and surprizing dismembring his Great *Monarchy*, and by the Surrendring an incredible number of large and rich *Provinces*, and many *Forts* and *Strong Towns* that were thought to be *Impregnable*.

And since there is so near a proximity between *Loo* and *Holland*, I cannot here omit to say somewhat of that *Great*, and *Considerable People*, among whom these *Gardens* are to be seen. But this Subject having been excellently well performed, if not in a manner exhausted, by one of the *best* of our *English Pens*, who has joined together the *Scholar* and the *Gentleman* in his Writings, as well as any of our Modern Authors; and particularly in his late *Essays* upon *Ancient* and *Modern Learning*, &c. I shall therefore refer my Reader to Sir *William Temple*'s Curious *Observations* upon the *United Provinces* of the *Netherlands*, for a more distinct and full knowledge of this Great Subject; and yet however I will not pass it by altogether in silence.

The *Belgæ*, or the *Low Countries*, were for their Valour and Courage eminent above other People, even in the time of *Julius Cæsar*, who at the beginning of his *Commentaries, de Bello Gallico*, has these Words. *Horum omnium fortissimi sunt Belgæ*.. When *Cæsar* had divided *Gaul* into three Parts, he says the Stoutest and most Couragious of them all, were the *Belgæ*, or *Low Countrymen*, then called *Gallia Belgica*, and since divided into *Seventeen Provinces* under the Dominion of the *House of Austria*, until *William* the Wise and Valiant *Prince* of *Orange*
first

first rescued, and the Invincible *Prince Maurice* of *Nassaw*, by abundance of Victories, and Sieges, compleated the Peace of *Seven* of those *Provinces*, and established them in a *Free Republick*, on the 9th of *April*, 1609. Again *Tacitus*, lib. 4. says, *Quicquid roboris apud Gallos sit, Belgas esse*: That the chiefest strength of all *France* was in these People. By which it appears, that the Dominion of *France* was then greater than it is now, and yet *Europe* was not over-run with it. That *Providence*, which certainly conducts and over-rules the Affairs of the World, sets bounds to *Empires*, as well as to the *Sea*. But to proceed, We have had, in the late War, sufficient experience of the Fortitude and Valour of the *Provinces* now mentioned. For what *Horse* have done their Duty, or fought better upon occasion than the *Walloons*, so miserable to look upon, usually called the *Spanish Horse*, though Natives of *Flanders*, and *Brabant*? Or what *Foot* have done better service in the late War than the *Dutch*, either in Sieges, or in Battels?

For if I were to speak of the *English Soldiery*, or were askt which were the *best Soldiers*, the *French* or the *Belga*, I should answer, the *English*: As Sir *Walter Rawleigh* did, when putting the question, in his Book of the World, which were the bravest Soldiers, the *Roman*, or the *Grecian*, made answer, the *English*; who, if they were in his time of such account and esteem, when only a *Queen*, though she indeed a most Excellent one, sate on the Throne, and left her Armies to the Conduct of her *Generals*: What admiration ought now to be had of the *English*, when they have our *Present King* at the *Head* of them! For we must not forget, *tanti esse Exercitum, quanti Imperatorem*. That the Strength of an *Army* is to be truly measured by the Valour and Conduct of the *General*.

And we may have some reason to doubt, whether *Alexander* the *Great*, had a better Army, or better Soldiers, even of his *Grecians*, with which it was his good Fortune to *Conquer the World* before him, and the which he led so boldly and bravely against a great concourse of *Persians*, who were a weak and effeminate People, than our *Edw.* the *Third*, or *Hen.* the *Fifth*, conducted against *France* it self, that was always esteemed a Warlike People, and was long ago adjudg'd such by *Cæsar* himself, by his own Experience, after he had *Conquered* them, and the rest of *Europe*. Those two famous *English Kings*, I say, did sufficiently manifest the *Superiority* of *English Armies* to all others, upon better trials than with *Persians*, when they had *Kings* at their *Head*, like to *themselves*, and *worthy* to *conduct them*.

The knowledge of this Truth, made the late Renowned and Excellent General *Turenne*, so much to covet *English Soldiers* before all others, and even before his own Countrymen, in the *Armies* he Commanded. And this made him so desirous of the Honour, to be called Father of the *English* when he was their Friend and Protector.

The last Demonstration we have had of the *English* undaunted Courage, was lately before *Namur*, where in the first *Attack* that was made, the

English Red-Coats struck such a Terror on the *French*, by an unparallel'd Bravery, that they were never able to recover themselves from the Fright, during the Siege. And when the Town was forced to Surrender, and the *King* then Ordered away all the *English* to the Succour of *Prince Vaudemont*, after the famous Retreat he had made, and to Preserve *Brussels* from falling into the hands of *Villeroy*, at the time he Bombarded It; the *Elector of Bavaria*, as I have heard, begg'd of His *Majesty* the detaining *Four English Battalions* towards carrying on the Siege of the *Castle*, and *Forts* adjoining, to the end that the same Terror might still remain with the Enemy, which the Valour of the *English* had struck so deeply upon them.

And of how great weight and force to the animating a People, or Army, the *Genius* of a *Good General* is, may be evinced, by that dismal *Revolution*, which happened to the *United Provinces* in the Year, 1672. This People, so famous in History for their *Courage*, and who had so gallantly signalized themselves for it against the *Spaniards*, when they were besieged by them in *Leyden*, *Haerlem*, and *Alcmar*; when it happened that the inundation of the *French* Armies came upon them in that Year, they made no manner of Resistance, their Towns hardly staid for a Summons to surrender, the *French* were advanced within sight of *Amsterdam*, and all the People of *Holland* seem'd to be without a Soul, as they were without a Head. Now at this so strange and fatal a Juncture, when once the *Perpetual Edict*, for abrogating the Office of *Stadtholder*, was annulled and at end, and the then *Young Prince* of *Orange* was restored to the *Power* and *Dignity* of his *Ancestors*, behold all things quickly recovered new Life, the Soldiers resumed the Courage they had lost, and the many *Towns* that were subjected to the *French*, in *Gelderland*, *Over Issel*, *Utrecht*, and in part of *Holland* it self, they were soon obliged to restore, and with the same celerity, as they had before over-run them. Nay, and the strong Town of *Grave*, situated upon the *Maese*, defended so well by *Chamilly*, and which the *French* were so unwilling to quit, was by the Vigour and prudent Conduct of the *same* successful *General*, our present most *August Monarch*; soon reduced to the Obedience of the *States*.

Moreover, to the same Cause, under *God*, to the Influence and Conduct of the *same General*, our most Magnanimous *King*, at the Head of the Confederate Army, *Spain* does now owe, not only the recovery of *Catalonia*, that was entirely lost; but the Preservation of *Brabant* and *Flanders*; by the Surrendring of *Aeth*, and *Courtray*; the Restitution of *Luxemburgh* and *Hainault*; and the late Conquest of *Namur* it self, in sight of a *French* Army of above a hundred thousand Men. And lastly, To the same *Generalissimo Europe* will ever

be

be indebted for this Glorious, and Wonderful *Peace*, that it now so happily enjoys, and which will always be recorded by Historians, to the immortal Praise of the *Great King William*, and to the Admiration of all Posterity.

The *Dutch* are not now torn and divided into Factions, and Parties, but are generally unanimous in their Counsels, calm in their Deliberations, and soon resolve on such Supplies or Taxes, as are necessary for the safety and welfare of the *State*. Formerly indeed, by the influence of *French Emissaries*, they have laboured under Divisions and Animosities, to the detriment, and danger of the *State*; and they have *not always hearkened to the wisest Counsel*, witness their hasty conclusion of the *Peace* at *Nimeguen*. But it is now become a frequent Observation among the *Dutch*, as a Gentleman of theirs of good understanding, and considerable employment, informed me, that in all things wherein they have been found to *follow* the *Wise Counsel* and *Advice* of *our present King*, they have *always* found themselves to be *successful*; and whensoever they have rejected, or *not followed* the same *Wise Counsel*, they have *as often* proved *unfortunate*, as the Events themselves have afterwards demonstrated. And hence it comes to pass, that now the *State* of the *War* for the next Year can there be determined in as *few days*, as it is *in months* in some other Countries. And now the *Pensionary* of *Holland* Consulting two or three days with the *Stadtholder*, does bring matters of the greatest moment to a shorter issue, than can be easily expected from the different Sentiments of a great number of Counsellours, though never so Wise.

Holland does contain a greater number of large, populous, and considerable Towns, than possibly are to be found so near together in any other part of the Universe. But though it abounds with multitudes of Inhabitants, and is enriched with so many great Towns, such as *Amsterdam*, the *Hague*, *Leyden*, *Dort*, *Delf*, *Rotterdam*, *Haerlem*, the *Briel*, &c. and others, as remarkable as the Chief Cities in other Countries, yet it yields to their sustenance little or no product of *Corn* or *Grain*. They are fain to fetch from the *Baltick*, and other Places, where it is plentiful, *Corn* enough to supply themselves, and their Neighbours, who want it. And they do send out great *Fleets* every year for that purpose. All this Country is a *low level*, lower than the *Sea* it self in many places, and defended from the inundation of the Sea by incredible *Dykes*, or *Banks*. All the *seventeen Provinces* are commonly called the *Low Countries*; not that they are all a *Low level* like unto *Holland*, but because they are situated towards the *Lower* part of the *Rhine*, and therefore are now called by Authors *Germania inferior*, or Lower *Germany*. The Country of *Holland*

land is excellent for *Pasture*, and cultivated to the best advantage by mighty labour and industry of the Inhabitants. They have cut large *Canals* through all parts of the Country, by means of which they do go commodiously and pleasantly from Town to Town, at a regulated easie expence, in cleanly and large Vessels, covered from the Weather, which set out constantly at certain hours, whether the Passengers are many or few, so soon as a *Bell* has done ringing. And by means of the said *Canals*, they do enrich, and water their Grounds at pleasure, and by Windmills they do throw out the water again, as they judge convenient. As we travel along these *Canals*, it is delightful to see so many Noble *Country Houses* bordering upon them, and adorned with neat *Gardens*, within sight of all Passengers. The water of these *Canals* is not offensive to the smell, even in the Summer time, although generally they are a standing Water. Possibly the great number of *Boats* that are continually plying to and fro, and drawn by Horses upon the trot, do keep the water in that agitation, that it has not time to putrifie, and grow offensive.

If this *Low Country* wants any thing, it is that *variety* of different Objects, which we do enjoy so much here in *England*; and the which *Variety* is so acceptable and agreeable to the nature of Mankind, who do all, and in every thing, consist of Variety, as in *Languages, Voices, Persons, Countenances, Gestures, Hand-writing, Cloaths, Appetites, Gustoes,* and what not. For what can contribute so much to the establishing our Healths, when declining into a Consumptive state, as Variety even of Country-Air? Or to what end has *Providence* made that infinite Provision of Flesh, and Fish, and all other Sustenance, if not to please and gratifie the different Appetites of Men? And I am mightily mistaken, if even in *Physick* too, the constant, long continuance of the *same Medicines* will have that good effect on abundance of Constitutions in Chronical Cases, as a Change, and Variety, and *Alteration of Medicines*.

But to return; there is little of our *Variety* to be seen in *Holland*. In travelling from place to place we do every where see the same sort of *Country* again and again. One House that we look upon may differ in dimensions, or other circumstances from another House; but the *Countrey* in one place has the same Aspect and Resemblance to that in another, as an Egg is like to an Egg. So that after our first Curiosity is reasonably well satisfied, our Entertainment in the Boats is commonly a Book, or viewing the mixt Company, or sometimes Discourse of I know not what, to pass away the time.

He that would see a kind of *Paradise* in this Country, must go by Land from *Dort* one League towards *Breda*; and there he will see all the way a Country so adorned with fine Houses, and fine Gardnes, and with

with that variety of Trees, planted in good order, and on all sides, that he will not know which way to cast his Eye first, so many Objects will invite him. Perhaps he will find himself distracted with as much diverting *variety*, as a young Gentleman or Lady is wont to be, when they first come out of the Country, and take the diversion of the *Ring* in *Hide Park*, in good Weather, on a *Sunday* Evening, when the Town is full. I need not describe the Charms, the Lustre, the Attractions of *Living Objects* there, Originals in the greatest perfection that Nature ever drew, and such Masterpieces of Man and Womankind, as neither *Italy* it self, nor all the World perhaps, can equal, or shew the like, as in this our *Paradise* of *Women*, as *England* has been often and justly called; nor need I hint how the Eyes of young Comers do there nimbly rowl about, not without pain sometimes, and even danger of Distortion.

The *Dutch Brabant* (to say nothing now of the *Veluwe*) from *Bergen-up Zoom* to *Breda*, *Boisleduc*, and so to *Grave*, is for much the greatest part a barren and sandy Countrey, where Horses do seldom travel above a League an hour. It is indeed a very strong *Frontier*, and hard to be attempted; and therefore the *French*, when they made their memorable Inroad on these *Provinces*, in the Year 1672. thought it more adviseable to hazard the difficult passage of the *Rhine* it self, by swimming one of the greatest Rivers of *Europe*, than to make its Attack upon any part of this large Frontier, where the Towns were so strong, and Forage would have been so scarce.

I was never in *Friesland*, nor *Groningen*, and therefore shall say nothing of those Parts. Once I rid from *Dieren* to *Zutphen*, over the *Issel*, in order to see a most Noble and Magnificent House of the Right Honourable the *Earl of Albemarle*, that his Lordship has lately built about half a League from *Zutphen*, and from which City there is a very spacious Avenue, or Access made to the *House*, between a double Row of Trees; his Lordship possessing a considerable Estate in that Province. This *House* has *Noble Gardens* adjoining to it, and made after the greatest Models, with *Terras-Walks*, *Fountains*, *Cascades*, *Canals*, &c. But they were not then finished, no more than the *House*, when I went to see them, after the last Campagne.

His *Lordship* is descended of an Ancient Family in this Country, and was *Baron* of *Keppell*, or *Kappell*, a Town of note in the Jurisdiction of *Zutphen*, before he was made an *English Earl*; and his Lordship is admitted among the Noblemen of *Holland*, which compose one part of the *States*, or have their Representation in the *States General*.

It is now twenty years since I was in *Zealand*, having been then sent to *Vlussing*, to see a sick Gentleman; whom after I had, through God's Blessing, soon put into a state of safety, I went to see *Middleburgh*: and
going

going thither upon a high Causeway, and looking down upon the Country, I could not but think it anciently belonged to the Dominion of the Sea, from whence it has therefore properly its Name of *Zeland*. They are Towns of great Trade, and Ships of the greatest Burthen, or Force, do ride in deep Canals, in the middle of the Streets of *Vlissing*, as well as in some parts of *Middleburgh*.

Great *Geographers*, may indeed write learnedly of all the World, though they never were out of the Country they were born in; nor ever hazarded their Persons, by dangerous Travels, in order to form their Notions, or Experience, Yet I shall give but a short and slender Account of my Observations in these Provinces, because my *Travels* here have been none of the greatest. I always thought it my Duty to continue in my proper Post, that so I might be ready to receive the Honour of the *King's Commands*, when His *Majesty* should judge it convenient to lay any upon me. For in my Profession sudden Accidents do sometimes happen, which will not allow that Liberty or Curiosity which other Gentlemen may take at pleasure.

Travelling abroad is certainly of singular use to the accomplishing a *Gentleman*. It enlarges all its Faculties, and takes off that narrowness or littleness of Mind, which for want of knowing the World, is apt to sowre his Temper and Conversation. It makes Men have just, and kind, and charitable Ideas of Mankind; and though many of our Gentlemen have so great and natural Endowments, and have besides such advantages above Foreigners, by their Education in our own Universities, that they do not seem to want either this, or any other Improvement; yet *Travelling* will, as it were, polish even a Diamond, take off its Roughness, and give it a new Lustre. And lastly, it will have that good effect, if it be well employed, as to make him *love his own Country the better*. And *Englishmen* that *Travel*, prove very unhappy, or make but little good use of it, if after they have seen what is to be seen abroad, they do not relish and admire the abundant Happiness of their own Country, much better than they did before.

A *Traveller* in *this* Country must be easy, and obliging in his Carriage, must make no noise, and but little dispute about his Reckonings; and then he will seldom have just cause of *Complaints*. He must be contented with what he finds upon the spot, and must take care to put his Host to as little trouble as may be. The more he appears a *Man of Quality*, the more he must expect sometimes to pay for it; but in the general, if he be prudent, and of a quiet peaceable Temper, he will Travel in *this* Country with as much frugality and fair dealing, as he can in any other, notwithstanding the Clamors which have sometimes been through the indiscretion of Strangers.

Great

Great Taxes are here suffered patiently, and without murmuring, for the sake of the *Liberty*, and *Security* they enjoy. They are all laid as equally as possible; and he that can invent a *New* and *Easy Tax*, that will not be Grievous to the People, shall be sure not to fail of a Publick Reward. Whatever is said of *Laws*, their *Taxes* are not like *Cobwebs*, in which the lesser Flies are usually catch'd, whilst the greater break through and escape. The inferior People, and the Rich, do pay to a Penny the same Pound-rate, in proportion to their Abilities. No body there thinks it their *Interest* (or at least it was never practised) to promote *Unequal*, or *Uneasy Taxes*, that shall crush one part with an insupportable burthen, and leave other parts free from feeling the weight. And their *Excesses*, although they reach almost every thing imaginable, are but little felt by the generality, or cause but few Complaints, by reason that all do share alike in the payments; according to their consumption; and that they reach the Luxurious and Expensive, more than the Poor, or Frugal People. Their having but one *Flesh Market*, and one *Fish Market*, &c. in a large Town, renders the Collection also easy and certain.

Justice is so well distributed among them, and severely executed, that many do think a Traveller may with more Safety pass through all the *seven Provinces* with his *Purse in his hand*, by Day and by Night, than go ten miles out of *London* with Money in his Pocket. Insomuch that few do suffer here on the account of *Felonies* and *Burglaries*, excepting some *Swart-makers* of late, who did blacken their Faces to conceal themselves in their Robberies. But that Gang has been happily discovered, and I think extirpated before this time. Those that ever Rob, or Steal, are all *hang'd* in *Chains* on the *Gallows*, or remain on the *Wheel* they were broke upon, until the Fowls of the Air have done picking their Bones, and they drop asunder. The which exemplary Punishment has that good effect in deterring others from the like Offences, that it is thought more do dye by the hands of the Common Executioner in *London* at one or two *Sessions*, than do on such accounts in a Year in all the *Seven Provinces*.

Though all Opinions, that are not Dangerous to the *State*, do here find a refuge, and are tolerated without scruple; yet *Idle People*, who will not work for a Livelihood, and have no visible way of subsisting honestly, will not long meet with a safe Sanctuary in these *Provinces*. The Magistrate will soon find them out, and make them give a probable account how they live and subsist. They who desire to see what becomes of *Idle Drones*, or *Profligate Wretches*, may take a walk to the *Rasp-houses*, and *Spin-houses*, where they will find them busily imployed at their daily Tasks; but if they will not work there according to appointment, the *Pump* is ready for the one to *Work* or *Drown*, and due Correction to enforce the other.

Indeed

Indeed the *Musick-Houses*, where loose People may meet in the Evenings, are suffered by Connivance, if not allowed by Authority, at *Amsterdam*, for some Politick Considerations, and particularly, that the *East-India* Seamen, or others, when they are troubled with *too much Money*, after a long Voyage, may here have the conveniency of disburthening, or soon ridding themselves of that *Incumbrance*; and may thereby be the sooner ready for *another Voyage*. But even *these Houses* do observe some Order. No boisterous Rudeness, or scandalous Obscenities are here permitted. And if a Couple do happen to agree Matters, strike up a Bargain, and resolve to try dangerous Experiments, they must e'en retire from thence to private Lodgings hard by, in order to commit their Follies. If in other Places of this famous *City* Frailties of this kind do come to be taken notice of; and the *Scout*, or *Magistrate*, who has his Spies abroad, should receive information of such Adventures, he enters all Places immediately without opposition, and where he finds Offenders, he inflicts such *Fines* and *Amercements* as will sufficiently discourage Debauchery; and the *Law* is soon dispatcht, being wholly in his own hands.

Their *Food* is commonly *Fish*, and they do generally seem to *like it*, and prefer it to *Flesh*, for Gusto, as well as Cheapness. For here they study not the Dainties of *Apicius*, nor the *Roman* or *Asiatick* Luxury. But in great Plenty they do live with great Frugality. Their *Flesh* they *Stew*, or *Boil*, and but seldom *Roast*. For their Fewel being *Turf*, they cannot so Conveniently, or so well *Roast*, as we do with our Coals and Wood. Their *Beer* and *Moll*, that are publickly sold, are wholesome, cool, and good, and fail not to quench the Thirst; whereas the Liquors we commonly meet with here in our *Inns*, and our *London Brewing* for Sale, is unhappily become such a *Mystery*, that a great deal of it will rather increase than quench the Thirst. Their *Nimmeguen Moll*, that is so plentifully transported about *Holland*, is a sort of *Oat-Ale*, much celebrated by them for its sanative Virtues, like their *Fresh Herring* in Summer. 'Tis a well-tasted, mild, and wholesome Ale. And 'tis hoped, that our *Parliaments*, when they have leasure to consider it, will take some care of the *wholsomness* of our *London Brewing*, both by *Brewers* and *Vintners*, since our *Health* does depend as much (if not more) upon the goodness of the *Liquors* we drink, as it does upon the *Food* we eat; since our Table-Beer, that is well Brew'd, is both a wholsome and pleasant Drink: And lastly, since we are come to that *Skill*, or Perfection now-a-days, that we can make *Wine* without *Grapes*, *Cyder* without *Apples*, and *Beer* without *Malt*.

The *Wine* they drink is either a sweet, and to us a nauseous *Whitewine*, which they call *French Wine*, but generally such *Whitewine*, as I cannot remember to have tasted in *France*; or else *Rhenish* and *Old Hock*. The *Rhenish* they are well known to make, or to store up plentifully, at

Dort;

Dort; and the *Hock* they have sometimes most excellent in its kind. For in cannot be supposed, that after so long a War on the *Rhine*, they can have that abundance of *those Wines* in reality, as whe the *Great Tun* of *Heydleburgh*, and other *Magazines* were in being, and the Vineyards not destroyed by the *Fate of War*. They have also common enough, a sort of *Sack*, or *Spanish Wine*; but it is as different from our *Canary*, as Posset-drink is from good Table-beer. *Claret* is no where to be found in their Publick Houses, unless perhaps at *Rotterdam*, or in some *French Ordinary*. And they are not yet fallen in love with *Claret*, or else in pure Civility to *England* do leave to us the free possession of a whole *Ocean* of *Claret*, fetcht from divers Countries and People, who are contented to drink *Water* themselves, and very *little Wine*, that we may have enough to drown our selves in, for pleasure and diversion. They have also every where their *Wormwood-wine*, which is commonly called by the Name of *Alsom Wine*, and by the *English* for sound sake *Wholesome Wine*, and the which they do not drink only for a Whet before Dinner, or on *Physical* accounts, but indifferently at any time of the Day, or Evening. It is made of the *French Wine* before-mentioned, and by its Bitterness does take off that lusciousness, or nauseous taste to Strangers.

This *Country* being Cold and Moist, their *Food* commonly *Fish*, their *Moll* very cool that they so much drink of, and their usual Wine *Rhenish* or *Hock*, their Temper easily chills and grows tender. Insomuch that they do as naturally fall into *Agues*, or else into *Putrid Fevers*, as we do into *Inflammatory* Distempers, or into the most *Violent* and *Malignant Fevers*, the effects of our Luxurious Living, and over-high Feeding. And although they have many Learned and Good Physicians among them, yet I know not how it happens, that *their Agues* are not very easily, or very soon Cured. Many Months are usually spent in such Cures, and the *Agues* very often first or last do turn into *Continued Fevers*, or from a Safe into a Dangerous State. For it happens that the use of the *Jesuits Bark* is too much suspected among them, and deserves not to be tried, until all other ways have been long tried in vain. And this I observe at a time, when there was never more general occasion of the using the *Bark*, and when the use of it was never more proper or effectual; I mean, in the *two first Campaigns* that I had the Honour to wait upon His *Majesty*, being the Years 1693, and 1694. *Agues* were at that time very *Epidemical*; and the *Continued Fevers* had such remarkable *Remissions*, that they were Cured with as much *Certainty*, if not Speed too, by the *Bark*, as the *Agues* themselves, provided that proper *Evacuations* did preceed its exhibitation. And I have reason to say with *Speed*, for I was then seldom obliged to above three or four Visits, even in those *Fevers*. And by reason of the *Barks* so well agreeing with the *Fevers* at that time, as well as the *Agues*, I made use of as many *Pounds* of the *Bark* in either of those two Years,

Years, as I have since done *Ounces* in my subsequent Campaign, or Summer; the *nature* of the *Fevers* being since quite *altered*, and therefore requiring a different Method of Cure.

And as for the common practice of the *Netherland Physicians*, in not using the *Bark* for the *Cure* of *Agues*, I am apt to believe, that it may have proceeded from a fear of *Innovation* in *Physick*, by a New Medicine of that importance. As it happened before to the Learned *Faculty* of *Paris*, who were as much afraid of *Innovations*, and all cried out *Fire*, when *Spagyrical Preparations* came first into use. For prudent Persons will not lightly relinquish an Established Method. And I can say farther in their behalf, that some few among them do begin to be convinced, that the *Bark* does not deserve to be too much neglected in the Cure of *Agues*. I may add concerning it, what is said of the *Italians*, *When they are Good, they are extraordinary Good; and when Bad, as extraordinary Bad*: So it may be said of the *Bark*, in what cases soever it is properly administred, no Medicine was ever known to have such great and good Effects; but when it is improperly, or unseasonably given, it becomes one of the most *Dangerous* that can be used. And therefore those who shall think fit to use this *Bark* in hazardous or difficult Cases, or in Asthmatick Persons, must be sure to have a very watchful Eye over it, to observe whether it agrees, or disagrees, and accordingly to prosecute, or quickly desist from its use.

But it may be *Objected*, That *Agues* are in some Countries more Dangerous in their Nature, and Difficult of Cure, than they are in others; as they are said to be with us in the *Hundreds* of *Essex*, and in the *Isle of Sheppey*. And therefore that the *Dutch* may have good reason for neglecting, or deferring, as they do, to Cure their *Agues* by the use of the *Cortex*, or *Bark*; and which possibly they do think will not agree so well with *their Agues*, or *their Tempers*, as it is found to do with *ours*.

To which I *Answer*, That when I was abroad, I never observed one single Person, either at *Loo*, or in the *Field*, who miss'd a Cure of his *Ague* by the use of the *Bark*, or who had any *Relapse* afterwards, that throughly followed my Directions, both before and after he had lost his Fits. And in that Success, I do think my self very much obliged to the Worthy Mr. *Rottermond*, Apothecary to His *Majesty's Person*, for his so good *choice* of the *Bark* I used, and who is perfectly skilful in the knowledge of Simples, and in all the parts of *Pharmacy*. Indeed some of His *Majesty's* inferiour Servants had *Relapses* through their own neglect and folly, because they would needs think themselves well before I did, and so soon as they had miss'd the *Fit*, would let me here no more of them until another *Fit* Returned; and this would sometimes happen more than once unto the same Person.

And

And however the *Bark* has been sometimes censured, as if the *Cures* by it were more subject to *Relapses* than by any other Methods; on the contrary, I am fully persuaded, that the *Cures* of *Agues* by *Vomits*, Seasonable *Purges*, by *Cordials acidulated*, or by *Amulets*, or *Domestick Applications* alone, are all more subject to *Relapses*, than those by the *Bark*, if this be prudently administred. To confirm which Opinion, I may add, That those who recover by the *Bark*, look florid and vigorous, grow quickly athletick and strong, and eat and digest well; whereas those who miss their *Fits* by other means, look pale and weakly some time after, and their natural Functions do return more slowly, and by degrees to their former strength and vigor.

As for our *Agues*, in the *Hundreds* of *Essex*, the Cure of the *Bark* does certainly agree with them, as well as with those in other Places. And it was to this very place that our once famous Sir *Robert Talbor* had his recourse, in order to the first establishing his Method of giving such repeated Doses of the *Bark*.

I do apprehend an *Ague* to be but a weak and flight Attack of a *Fever*, or to be an imperfect *Fever*, or it may be said to be a *Fever by halfs*. Either the Enemy that makes the Assault is weak and feeble, or the Fort that Nature defends is Strong, and well prepared to make Resistance. Either the Body is not sufficiently predisposed for such a Combustion as the *Continued Fever* does occasion, or the *Pores* are then but *little Obstructed* and therefore after the two first proper Symptoms of a *Fever*, the *Coldness* or Shivering, and the *Burning Heat*, have a while exerted themselves, there is always in an *Ague* a sudden succession of a Profuse *Sweat*, which terminates the *Fit*. For when the *Burning* still remains, and no *Sweat* succeeds, the *Fever continues* of course, and undergoes another denomination.

The one may be said to make its Impression more *Outwardly*, and upon the *Pores*; the other not only so, but also more *Inwardly*, and upon the *Vitals*. The one falls chiefly upon the *Outworks*, or upon the *Counterscarp*, the other makes a breach in a *Bastion*, or in the *Curtine*. The Attack of the one is not in it self hazardous or dangerous to the State of the Body; the Attack of the other is like a *General Assault*, and proves of a *Critical* nature, or determines the fate of *Life* and *Death*. And this is a more easy, and natural, and a more intelligible explication of the General Difference between *Fevers* and *Agues*, than other Accounts of them, that are more Obscure and Intricate, more Philolosophical, or artificially wrought into some Ingenious *Hypothesis*.

I have observed, that in *Seasons* or Times when *Agues* are very Epidemical, as it is in *Countries* where they are very common and frequent, the *Continued Fevers* are usually of the same nature and progeny, and do generally require a like Method of Cure, and are actually cured by a

prudent

prudent use of the *Cortex*, as *Intermittent Fevers*, or *Agues* are. Only in the former we must always remember, as we must also sometimes in the latter, to take care that we use sufficient proper *Evacuations*, in order to bring the small *Remission* that they then commonly have, to some *Intermission*, if it can be obtained, before we presume to give the *Bark*. And then we may as safely and effectually make use of the *Bark* in the first, as we do without difficulty in the other. I hope the Reader will excuse this Digression, because, with respect to my Faculty, it may be matter of Note and Illustration to some, if not of Use and Benefit also to the Publick.

The Diet and Air of the *Dutch* do much contribute to their growing so plump, and fat; and that may be one reason, why they *Bleed* so sparingly, and seldom as they do. For when they do think fit to *Bleed*, they will seldom or never take away more *Blood* from a Man or Woman, than we do from an *Infant* of a Year old. How they came to fall into such an Extremity of *Bleeding little*, I cannot well comprehend, considering how profusely the *French*, and the more Southern Nations, do use *Venesection* upon most occasions. Nor are the *Dutch* the most abstemious from *Wine* and *Brandy*, which will be apt to heat and inflame the Blood, and consequently upon excess sometimes cause *Diseases* that properly require *large Bleedings*; neither am I ignorant that their *Physicians* are very *Learned Men*, and must read those Excellent Books of *Galen*, concerning *Venesection*.

Coughs, that are so common with us, are very seldom known among the *Dutch*; insomuch that in the *Autumn*, when we are *deafning* one another with *Continual Coughing*, you may go into a *Church* there, and not hear a single person *Cough*. And for this reason I am induced to think, when an *Inflammation* there falls upon the *Lungs*, and causes a *violent Cough*, they cannot so well deal with such a strange and *foreign Disease*, as those who have less apprehensions of *Bleeding plentifully* when there is occasion.

I have been ask'd sometimes the reason, why *Holland* has so few, or *No Coughs*, and *England* so many. The True Reason I conceive to be this: *Holland* has as great a scarcity of *Minerals*, as of *Corn*, of its native growth. *England* does abound with *Minerals* of divers Kinds, that are very offensive to the *Lungs*; howsoever *Chymists* may commend the *Preparations* from them, for other Physical uses. And our *Air* does abound with *Mineral Effluviums*, and much of our *water* with *Mineral Impregnations*. This is also the reason, why the *Isle* of *Sheppey*, otherwise a Rich Countrey, is so unwholesome to live in. And this is the reason, why the Waters of the *Danube*, and other Rivers in *Hungary* are so unhealthful to drink of. For it was well said of *Pliny*, the Great Naturalist: *Tales sunt Aquæ, quales Terræ per quas fluunt.*

I cannot omit to take some notice of the *good Provision* they do make for their *Poor*, whereby they are not pester'd or molested in their Streets, in their Shops, in their Coaches, with any crowd of Beggars, which would serve to divert their *Charity* from proper and good Objects; I mean poor Labourers, or Housekeepers, who take much pains, to the getting little, towards a sorry maintenance of a great many Children; or such who through Infirmities, or Accidents, are disabled from getting any thing at all, and are above the *Trade* of *Begging*. If the *Poor* there cannot work, or do want work, there is provision made for them both. The *Magistrate*, or *Officers*, do not think it any *trouble* to them, to go sometimes from House to House, to enquire privately into their Condition, to observe what Children they have, and to understand what they can, or cannot do, towards their Maintenance. And accordingly, both the *known*, and *unknown Poor*, who are ashamed to ask for what they want, are supplied by the *Publick* from time to time.

In their *Churches* they do never assemble to serve *God*, but they manifest their *Love* to their *Neighbour*. There is always a *Bag* transmitted to every person, with the notice of a little *Bell*; and I am told, that there's hardly one single Person, though never so mean, or little, that comes to *Church*, but does drop some *Mite*, or *Doit*, into the *Poor's Bag*, every time he comes. And whatsoever is so collected, or upon other Occasions, for the *Poor*, does not serve to fatten, and make merry, the Petty Officers, but is faithfully accounted for, and expended duly to its proper Uses.

The *Apparel* of the *Dutch* is grave and free from levity. The Men do put on *Black* on Sundays, and other high days; and at other times dark Colours. And this is the mode of all Citizens, and many others, even of the Boors, not only in the *Seven Provinces*, but in *Brabant*, and *Flanders*. Nevertheless, their *Nobility* and *Gentry*, both Men and Women, do dress as fine, and modishly, as we our selves, or others, that cannot for all the world help imitating or *Apeing* the *French*.

Indeed I must say, we in *England* are not in such mighty haste for *New Fashions*, but that we can make a shift to stay until our *Taylors* do supply us, and make us happy with *Modes* from *France*, by their taking a Journey on purpose to *Paris* in vacation-time. But some of the *Princes* of *Germany* are more careful to be *à la mode de France* as early as may be; for they have the *Fashions* brought to them some hundred Leagues in Post-haste; and, before the War, did use to keep *Couriers* at *Paris* ready, to bring them quickly matters of such great moment, upon the *first Invention* of a *New Mode*. As if *Peace* and *War*, or a sudden irruption on a Neighbour-State, could not be of greater concern, than a new-cut Feather in the Cap, or some surprizing Master-piece of Gayety.

And

And thus I have but gently toucht upon some of the *Customs*, and some part of the *Good Government* of the *Dutch*, which though in so near a Neighbour-State, they cannot but be well known to many of our *better sort*, who are perfectly well acquainted with this part of the World, and much better than they can be informed by me; yet I thought even the mentioning these things would not be unacceptable to some others, who have never been abroad. For if I should undertake the Relation at large of only the *Curiosities* of *Amsterdam* it self, or should particularly speak of the *Keyser-Graft*, the *Princes Graft*, and the *Heer-Graft*, three spacious Streets that do almost incircle the whole *City*, and three Streets that contain more Sumptuous Houses, all of Stone, throughout their long circuit, than can be well imagined by those who have not seen them; or if I should treat of the Pleasant and Magnificent Gardens of *Sorgvliet*, within a Mile of the *Hague*, given some years since by His *Majesty* to the Right Honourable the *Earl* of *Portland*, and which no Strangers, that have any Curiosity, can omit Seeing; they are so Admirable and Pleasant: and the *King* does often retire thither to dine, whilst he resides at the *Hague*; or lastly, if I should describe the Charming Sweetness of the *Hague*, in the Summer-time, the Pleasantness of *Leyden*, or enter into a repetition of what others have done with applause before, this Account would soon swell into a *Volume*, and a short *Memorandum* into a *prolix Narration*.

To conclude, The *Dutch* do deserve a great Consideration and Kindness from us, as they are become a Principal *Bulwork* of the *Protestant Religion*, next unto *England*, whose *Church* is without Dispute the chiefest *Honour* and *Glory* of the *Reformation*, and the brightest *Example* of *True Moderation*, between the gay Decorations and Paintings of *Superstition* on the one side, and the mean and homely Addresses to *Divine Majesty* on the other. And now especially the *Dutch* may lay nearer claim to our Amity, when the *Protestant Interest* in general had never greater need of *Bulworks* and *Defences*; when not only *France* does manifest an unparalell'd *Bigotry* by an impolitick and unchristian Rage and Persecution, that may in time be found so to weaken and unpeople it self, as to be a *main cause* of her Declension, whatsoever glorious or formidable appearance she may make for the present; but also divers *Roman Catholick Princes* have with one accord, and with an unusual Sympathy, in this Age, exerted a *Zeal* against their *Protestant* Subjects, that is inconsistent with their own *Temporal Interest*, and contrary to the Rules of *Humanity* or *Prudence*.

And 'tis certain, that whenever *Religion* comes to be so far abused, as to lay aside the most Essential part of it, *Charity*, it blinds the Eyes of all *Zealots*, that they cannot see their own *Interest*; it transports and turns them from all the Rules of *Prudence* and *Reason*, and makes

Men

Men commit the most fatal, and extravagant *Errors*, in Politicks and Civil Society.

It is worth the Consideration of warm and imprudent Princes, whose indiscreet Zeal is so apt to instigate them to molest and harass their Subjects for the sake of what Honest and Pious Men cannot sometimes help, I mean, difference in *Religious* Sentiments, what happened to the Observation of *Charles* the *Fifth*, after he had resigned the *Empire* to his Brother *Ferdinand*, and the *Kingdom* of *Spain* to his Son *Philip* the *Second*. This Warlike and Great Prince, after he was grown weary of the Pomp and Glories of the World, and had made his *Retreat* into a *Monastery*, had abundance of *Clocks* brought him thither by the best Artists he could hear of; and his desire was to make all his *Clocks* strike together at the same Hour. When he had long tried this Attempt in vain, he brake out into this *pious* Exclamation: *How vain and foolish is it for Princes to endeavour to make all their Subjects to be of one mind, when no Art is able to make a few Clocks strike together at the same time!*

And therefore, since now no former Alliances, no common Interest, no remembrance of Benefits lately received, no Obligations, how great soever, can possibly restrain *Roman Catholick* Potentates from trampling their own Subjects under their feet, meerly for thinking otherwise than they do in matters of *Superstition*, and from attempting to *Convert* them by the powerful mission of irresistible *Dragoons*, and by more refined Methods than were heretofore practised in the Ten dull Pagan Persecutions; most certainly a *Hearty Union*, and Strict Alliance, and *Friendship*, between *England* and *Holland*, was never more absolutely necessary than at this time, for the Good and Prosperity, shall I say, or for the Preservation and mutual Defence of *both Nations*, and also for the maintenance and support of the *Protestant Interest* throughout *Europe*. Whilst *We* stand firm, and strictly *United* with *Holland*, we shall have no need to fear the Power or Attempts of *any Common Enemy*; our *Trade* can never suffer in any great degree, and our *Riches* will supply to us such *Sinews* of *War*, such an inexhaustible *Magazine* of *Military Force*, as will defeat and overcome those *Princes* or *Monarchs*, whose *Ambition* will never suffer them to be *quiet*, but whilst they are *disturbing* the *Peace* of their *Neighbours*, or who will needs be aiming at *Impossibilities*, the *Philosopher's Stone*, or *Universal Monarchy*.

FINIS.